PHOTOSHOP Fine Art Cookbook

PHOTOSHOP
Fine Art Cookbook
for digital photographers

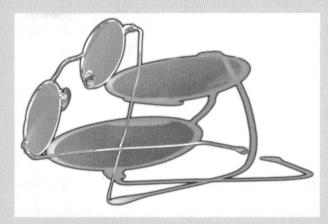

John Beardsworth

ILEX

Contents

PHOTOSHOP FINE ART COOKBOOK
Copyright © 2006 The Ilex Press Limited

First published in the United Kingdom in 2006 by:

I L E X
The Old Candlemakers
West Street, Lewes
East Sussex BN7 2NZ

I L E X is an imprint of The Ilex Press Ltd

Visit us on the Web at:
www.ilex-press.com

This book was conceived by:

I L E X
Cambridge, England

ILEX Editorial, Lewes:
Publisher: Alastair Campbell
Managing Director: Stephen Paul
Creative Director: Peter Bridgewater
Managing Editor: Tom Mugridge
Project Editor: Adam Juniper
Art Director: Julie Weir
Designer: Alistair Plumb
Design Assistant: Kate Haynes

ILEX Research, Cambridge:
Development Art Director: Graham Davis
Technical Art Director: Nicholas Rowland

British Library Cataloguing-in-Publication Data
A catalogue record for this book is available from the British Library.

ISBN 10 – 1-904705-74-X
ISBN 13 – 978-1-904705-74-1

Printed and bound in China

For more information on this title please visit:
www.web-linked.com/phofuk

INTRODUCTION

By chance, or after hours of careful planning, many camera enthusiasts find themselves asking, "Is this the exact spot?" Is this where Ansel Adams placed his tripod, or Claude Monet set down his easel? There are also moments when you are far from the Yosemite Valley or Monet's spectacular garden in Giverny, France, but the Dolomites or those New York water lilies appear to be exactly the sort of scene that Adams or Monet would have picked to photograph or paint. It could also be something so wonderfully kitsch that it seems to belong in a Martin Parr photograph; some sunflowers in an old vase; or the sun that sets so blindingly over the harbor that it makes you think of the J.M.W. Turner paintings you saw exhibited last year.

The photograph you take might be pretty good—even close to the style you imagined. But it remains a digital color photograph, not the fine-toned black-and-white image with a great dark sky and clearly defined clouds that you're really after. It's not an oil painting with Van Gogh's great swirling brushstrokes. But it does have potential.

This book is about using the power of Photoshop to make the most of that potential.

The book is laid out in four main sections. The Artist's Eye is about pausing to review a picture before you start imitating its style. You don't have to be a trained artist—simply enjoying photography and art is enough. What subjects would the original artist typically photograph or paint? Is there a characteristic composition or viewpoint? Which colors or tones would make your picture allude to a well-known style? Are there textures or physical qualities that you can include in your picture? While few artists are limited to one type of work, pausing for reflection will help you appreciate their work and give you a clearer idea of what you are attempting to achieve.

The Tricks of the Trade is an overview of Photoshop's tools and the ways of working that are most likely to help you get within spitting distance of your goal. Without assuming any level of Photoshop experience, this section explains how to use tools to select image areas, and filters and adjustments to transform the appearance of your selection. It also discusses ways to work efficiently and flexibly, so you can easily retrace your steps and refine your approach as your confidence grows.

The heart of the book is found in the two sections entitled Photographers and Painters & Printmakers. Here you'll find "recipes" for recreating a wide range of individual photographic and artistic genres, styles,

ABOVE Until the arrival of Photoshop, photomontage was a skilled and time-consuming task. Much of the work was done in the darkroom, exposing different negatives in sequence. Now we can do it on the desktop.

LEFT The silkscreen technique was popularized by Andy Warhol's images of subjects ranging from canned soup to Elvis Presley. You can follow in Warhol's footsteps with the Silkscreen project in this book.

and techniques from the artistic traditions of Europe and North America. Each recipe introduces a particular style or technique, its historical and artistic context, and its principal exponents—the names you might research in books or on the Internet to help gain greater insight into the style. After assessing its key visual and physical qualities, a series of easy-to-follow steps shows how you might manipulate your image to make it resemble the chosen style.

Improvisation is vital. You may want to make an authentic reproduction, or have fun imagining how 21st-century New York might look as a Daguerreotype or painted by Canaletto. There's nothing to stop you from experimenting.

Learning about the original technique and its context often sparks an idea when you're struggling to imitate its appearance in Photoshop. It can also have other creative results. Much as I love visiting

ABOVE Futurism first emerged in Italy in the early 20th century. Futurist art utilized tightly cropped images of machines, often superimposed on others, to create an impression of speed and power.

RIGHT Using closely cropped images and some simple Photoshop color adjustments, it is possible to recreate the feel of the Art Deco flower photography of the 1920s and '30s.

galleries, I don't paint or draw. But writing this book did lead me to try cyanotype printing—a 19th-century photographic process—with materials you can buy in kit form. You make a large negative in Photoshop, use your inkjet printer to output it onto overhead transparency film, coat some paper with the chemicals, and expose it to sunlight. So far I'm just experimenting, learning, and having fun. So go ahead—surprise yourself with your creativity!

THE ARTIST'S EYE

Analyzing pictures
and identifying their
special characteristics

Subject matter

The subject matter of a picture is most likely the first characteristic you notice. Does the photographer specialize in wilderness landscapes or candid street-life images? Does the painter depict North Atlantic storms, or dignify aristocrats and bishops? Mention Degas and you probably think of ballerinas, while for Robert Mapplethorpe it's male nudes.

First impressions, however, can be misleading, and a little research often changes what you think is typical of an artist. For example, the French artist Georges Seurat, famous for his theory of color vision known as Pointillism, is best known for two waterside scenes—yet he painted many more coastal views, as well as a number of paintings of ballerinas and circuses. Similarly, the Japanese woodcut master Katsushika Hokusai is famous for his landscapes featuring Mount Fuji, but of course many more of his works don't feature this iconic volcano. Indeed, the war photographer Don McCullin has also shot some awe-inspiring landscapes, while Mapplethorpe created wonderful pictures of flowers.

Photographs and paintings inevitably reflect the fashions and technology of their day. You wouldn't expect motor vehicles in Thomas Cole-style images, or advertising billboards in a "Canaletto." Such anachronisms can be made less obvious with careful use of Photoshop filters, or you can try to shoot images that already resemble traditional subject matter—photographing an old church from a position where trees hide the mall parking lot, for example.

On the other hand, it can be instructive to play around with the concept of authenticity. Van Gogh may never have visited the Great Plains, but how might he have painted your tree-lined street? Take it one step further—how might he have painted the downtown diner where you shelter from the rain? It won't be quite as convincing as a cornfield or an old chair, but that's half the fun.

Apart from your own bookshelf, the Internet is an easy way to confirm or overturn your impressions of an artist's work. At the back of this book I've included a few useful links to major art galleries in North America and Europe.

Historical reenactment events make great photographic subjects for Old Master-style paint effects.

They built a Venice in the Nevada desert— so why not give it the Canaletto treatment?

Composition and the angle of view

Composition is the way in which the elements of a work of art are combined and work together to create the whole. Emulating an existing composition can help your manipulated photograph reflect its artistic inspiration—the 18th-century English artist J.M.W. Turner alluded to the 17th-century French painter Gellée Claude in a similar way. And, even if you don't yet feel entirely confident about analyzing paintings, an interest in photography is a good starting point.

It's likely many of the questions will be obvious to you already. Where does the artist usually place the horizon? Dead center? Or is there evidence of the Golden Rule or the Rule of Thirds? If you have not come across this before, it's simple: break up your image into a grid by dividing each side into thirds and drawing lines between those points. The image is then composed so interesting features are at the intersections of those lines, or run along them.

Is the composition closed at the sides? Claude's seaports show tall buildings at either side, which hold the eye inside the painting, while its subdued colors give his work a sense of order befitting the idealized Classical scenes. Turner's *Dido Building Carthage*

deliberately imitates these devices, but this is not typical of his later works. Don't just look for physical subjects around the edges of a picture. For example, in his darkroom, Ansel Adams burned in (darkened) the edges of his prints to achieve a similar effect.

Where are the major lines in an image? Grant Wood's landscapes often use highways, another subject familiar to photographers, as lead-in lines.

What graphical qualities can you identify in a painting? Are objects framed within other objects? Are certain patterns repeated, like the circles and the volcano-shaped triangles in some Hokusai works? Or does the artist clamp a structure of vertical and horizontal lines or planes onto the subject?

Where is the light source? Is the image backlit? Is the light diffuse or harsh, direct or ambient?

With portraits, how does the artist portray his subjects? Is the image full body, from the waist up, or cropped to the face? Is the top of the head included?

Look at the angle of view. It's a bit tougher with painters, who have more freedom to create an artificial sense of perspective, but Van Gogh strikes me as preferring a wider angle than the Impressionists. For photographers, try to identify

ABOVE The Rule of Thirds—the main point of interest, in this case the man's eyes, is placed along the line marking the top third, and close to the intersection of two lines.

LEFT Whistler was heavily influenced by Japanese art and tried using a rectilinear pattern in his nocturnes, similar to the one made by this breakwater.

LEFT This picture's angle of view is narrow and the background is out of focus. In this case I used a zoom lens at 320mm (efl).

ABOVE This picture has a wide angle of view and puts you close to the center of the action. My focal length was 28mm (efl).

the type of lens that was used. If it's a wide-angle lens, your eye is led in many different directions, and nearby objects appear relatively large. Or does the photographer favor a long lens that flattens perspective and depth of field?

One sometimes reads that a photographer took a picture with a particular lens—Cartier-Bresson, for example, reputedly stuck to one lens, a 50mm. Try the specified focal length on your camera and see if it creates pictures with a similar angle of view.

A point to remember is that most digital SLR cameras have sensors smaller than 35mm film, so divide by a factor of 1.5–1.6. Cartier-Bresson's 50mm lens would be roughly equivalent to a 35mm on a digital SLR. Since the sensor dimension varies, photographers find it easier to describe their lenses in terms of the 35mm "equivalent focal length," or efl, rather than the specific dimension of the lens in question. (This argument is rendered academic, of course, if you use a camera like the Canon EOS-5D with a sensor the same size as 35mm film.)

You can often glean a large amount of information from the writings of experienced art critics, or simply from the description that accompanies a picture in a gallery or website. Add this knowledge to your interest in photography, and you're already equipped to analyze any type of image.

13

Color palettes and tonal balance

As with composition, the photographer's eye is already well attuned to analyzing the typical color and tonal balance of any picture. It probably won't take you long to decide that a John Constable landscape features rich, natural greens, while Henri Matisse favored wild, unrealistic colors. A John Marin New England seascape only contains cold blues and grays, while Hokusai used a Prussian blue pigment that had recently become popular. A Caravaggio might be very dark but has red accent colors and golden candlelight, while British artist L.S. Lowry's paintings of cities in northern England were an industrial gray. Instead of identifying which colors are present, it can provoke more thought if you ask yourself which colors are absent in a work.

People new to black-and-white photography often make the mistake of thinking that black and white is just like turning down the color on the TV. Look more closely and you see that landscape photographers such as Ansel Adams show dark skies and clearly defined clouds—not because they were lucky with the weather, but because they used colored lens filters. Tonal range varies—Adams's prints typically contain a full range of tones with many intermediate shades, while Bill Brandt's tend to have much higher contrast. Also look for grain—photojournalists such as Don McCullin needed faster, grainier film, while the grain is barely visible in the work of larger format and studio photographers. And look, too, for the tone, which may not be neutral black and white, but a very subtle sepia tone that would be typical of platinum printing paper.

Other important physical qualities may only become evident when you examine the original painting in a gallery or handle the photographic print. Reading about an artist's technique, you may learn that he or she applied thick oil paint in heavily laden brushstrokes—but this won't be obvious in images printed in books or viewed online. Daguerreotypes, for example, were made on silver plate, and you really need to see one in a museum to fully appreciate it.

It's not possible to physically reproduce the surface texture of an oil painting in a digital print. Instead, you will need to rely on changing the image

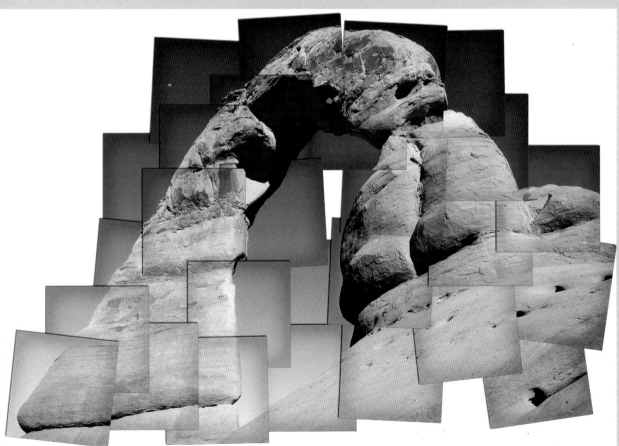

ABOVE While one can imitate a cyanotype's tone, careful choice of printing paper can also give the impression of chemicals impregnating the paper rather than forming a surface. For this picture I chose a matte surface and a textured art paper, not a glossy finish.

LEFT Polaroid "joiners" consist of overlapping instant prints. Imitate this by varying the darkness around the edge of each tile.

quality, perhaps using Photoshop's Paint Daubs filter and exaggerating the effect. Printing onto one of the wide variety of art papers available today can also add texture to your pictures.

Another physical quality to bear in mind is the size of your image. You may not be able to match the dimensions of large-scale canvases, but in other cases you can increase the illusion of authenticity by printing at an appropriate size. Cartes de visites, for example, were intentionally small and cheap, and were displayed in albums with two or more cut-out windows. People wrote their names on them, too.

ABOVE Cold grays and blues suit this shot of the Atlantic coast, and were also typical of U.S. artist John Marin's New England coastal scenes.

LEFT This homage to Dali was easy to create with Photoshop's Warp tool, introduced in version CS2.

THE TRICKS OF
THE TRADE

An overview of the
digital artist's tools
and techniques

Shooting for digital manipulation

If you want to imitate a well-known work in a "realistic" style, it's obviously a lot easier to shoot a similar subject as your starting point. If French photographer Eugène Atget is your hero, start by taking a picture in Paris, or go to "Constable country" if you want to capture the 19th-century painter's customary scenery. There is still digital work to do, but it's mainly post-production fine-tuning.

It's a different matter when you shoot a picture to provide raw graphic material for a less-realistic artistic style, or to add details to a composition. Think of it as walking along the beach collecting driftwood for a sculpture in a house you're still only hoping to buy. You don't necessarily need to make much effort if you intend to tear the image apart in Photoshop and stretch, filter, and recycle the bits. I have deliberately kept some original photographs very low-tech, with the kitchen table and late afternoon sun the closest I've come to using a studio. Other equipment included sheets of white paper or newspaper as reflectors to lift the shadows, and beer bottles to prop up a box and improve the angle of the sunlight.

When seeking a location for your shoot, look for a plain background with a color that contrasts with the subject. This applies particularly to "studio" shots where you control the environment—but when shooting outdoors, try to find an angle that will make the background easier to select and remove. Another tip is to use a longer lens and open up the aperture, throwing the background out of focus.

Of course, Photoshop can be used to add various textures to photographs, to age them, or simulate some other technique. But why create artificial textures when it's just as simple to use File > Import and use your scanner to acquire all sorts of interesting material that's lying around the house? I've used an assortment of business envelopes, fresh and torn, and sandpaper. It's also a great idea to buy variety packs of art paper. Before trying them on your inkjet printer, scan each one and add it to your digital library. Once you have the basic texture, you can filter and distort it in Photoshop.

This guitar was destined to become a Cubist still life. I made three quick snaps for raw material—in fact, I spent longer brushing off the dust than I did taking the photos.

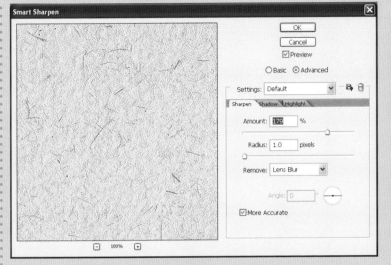

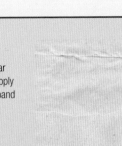

Manila envelopes have surprisingly interesting textures, and they also tear and fold nicely. You can apply filters in Photoshop to expand the range of textures.

Here I planned to depict the asparagus realistically and chose the red box as a background because its plain, contrasting color would be easy to select and delete.

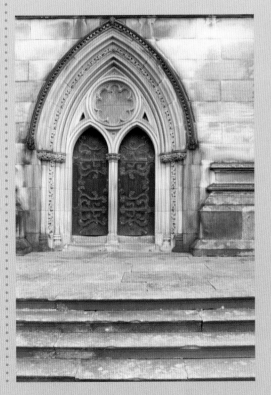

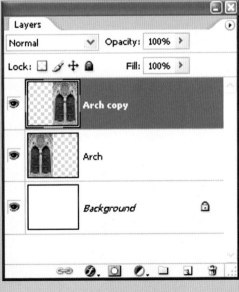

It's easy to create libraries of raw material. This arch can be copied and extended into a series of windows.

Digital workflow

So you're back from Yosemite, where you and thousands of others found Ansel Adams's exact viewpoints. Or you've been out all day with your digital camera and returned with an inventory of pictures for assembling your Matisse—maybe a Fernand Léger, too, afterward, if you're not too tired. The door's closed, the coffee's fresh, Photoshop's open. Ready to go?

Well, not quite. First of all, copy your originals. I don't want to labor this point, but take a moment to make sure there is no way you can overwrite your original photographs. This stricture applies especially if you shoot using the JPEG or TIFF formats. If your pictures are in a Raw file format, Photoshop does all it can to prevent you overwriting the original file. But there are ways—so don't take the risk.

When you're sure your originals are backed up, it's time to move your coffee cup well away from the keyboard, straighten your back, and get to work.

It may sound obvious, but always try to start out with a plan. Sometimes you know exactly what steps to take, but even then it's worth doing a few dummy runs. The Photoshop "Polaroid emulsion lift" (see pages 106–7) happened exactly this way. I had to try many approaches, and mostly they were dead ends, so it was worthwhile to work roughly until I had the bright idea and the final method came together. So, do a dummy run to test your concept, and then return to the beginning and work more carefully on the final masterpiece.

Once the idea is there, although the exact steps will vary widely, the process is usually the same:

● Work in layers, so you don't destroy the original image at the bottom of the layer stack.

● Use adjustment layers to change image color and contrast.

● When you need to destroy pixels, paint with the brush or apply a filter on a separate layer, or stretch and warp a copy of the image layer.

This "non-destructive" layer-based method is essential for this sort of work, and allows you to easily backtrack and try another approach or fine-tune the effect later. One layer may simply be used to mimic the type of paper or other material used for the original photographic or painting technique. It's even better, however, if you can print on realistically textured paper and find a frame to match your finished product.

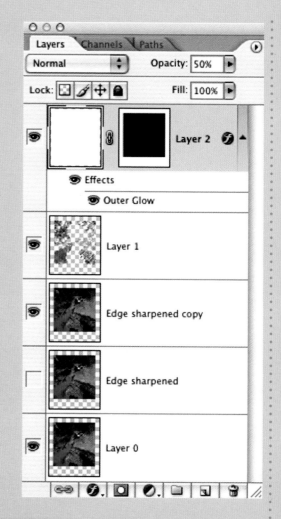

20

ABOVE Remember to take full advantage of Photoshop's layers in order to preserve data as you progress.

LEFT It took a lot of dummy runs to get this close to the look I was after. It often makes sense to work on reduced-size images so Photoshop processes faster and your experimentation is more productive.

Thinking about the "real" process helps you work out how to recreate it in Photoshop. In an actual Polaroid emulsion lift, the emulsion layer is soft, wet plastic, which sometimes twists and folds when it is pressed onto art paper. The folds are an accurate color, but multiplied. These were the clues to how to achieve the effect.

Layers and working non-destructively

I know of at least one former darkroom enthusiast who prefers to work in Photoshop without ever using layers. He uses the Dodge and Burn tools directly on the image, just as before, and changes image contrast by using Image > Adjustments > Curves. He's not saving disk space or processing power—quite the contrary—but it simply feels natural, and it works for him.

But in each case, when he saves and closes the file, the pixels in the original image are changed forever. Destroyed. So, instead of dodging and burning on the image, do so on a layer. You can duplicate the layer to double its strength. You can fine-tune its impact by reducing its opacity, or remove it entirely. Don't use Image > Adjustments > (I almost add the word "ever"). It's better to change the contrast with a Curves adjustment layer—you have the same flexibility when

you return to your desk a month later, and you can also copy it onto other images. Layers also have masks, which you can paint so that each layer's effect is targeted to certain areas of the image. Furthermore, adjustment layers have styles that allow you to change their appearance by adding gradients, colors, outlines, drop shadows. If you are destroying pixels, use layers.

Working non-destructively in Photoshop gives you the ability to change an image's pixels, save your work, close down your computer, and get on with life for a while. When you return to the image, you'll be able to fine-tune it, or maybe backtrack and advance again, but this time up a different slope. Layers are the key to this way of working, and they are used extensively throughout this book.

Photoshop CS2 allows you to use Ctrl/Cmd-Click to select more than one layer, by clicking each layer

near its name. This enables you to apply changes to more than one layer at a time. If you Ctrl/Cmd-Click the layer's thumbnail, you create a selection of just the pixels on that layer, not the transparent areas. Another option is to Alt/Opt-Click the thumbnail—this makes just that layer visible, while another Alt/Opt-Click restores the other layers' visibility. In other words, layers are efficient, too.

While there is always more than one "best" way to work in Photoshop, when you're imitating artists' styles there can be a lot of trial and error—or improvisation. You might be "doing a Renoir" and then realize the image is very Hogarth. Even experienced users continually learn new tricks, so don't be put off if you seem to have taken the wrong route—simply retrace your steps and get on with it. Working non-destructively is the only way to work.

22

LAYERS MENU

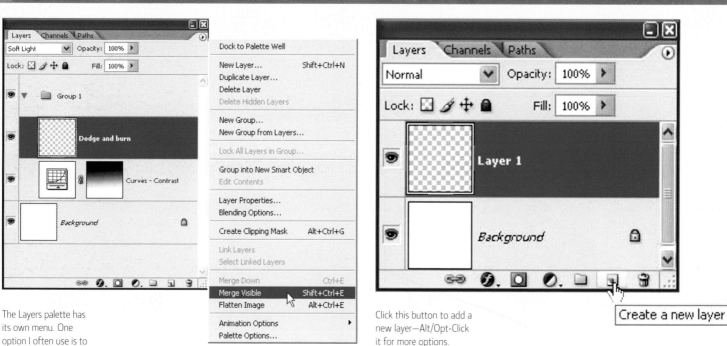

The Layers palette has its own menu. One option I often use is to hold down the Alt/Opt key and select Merge Visible. In Photoshop CS2, this creates a new layer, but earlier versions of the program make you first create a new layer into which to merge the others.

Click this button to add a new layer—Alt/Opt-Click it for more options.

Create a new layer

ADJUSTMENT LAYERS

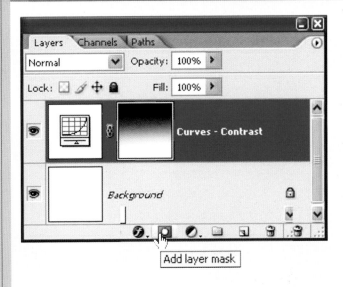

Create new fill or adjustment layer

Use an adjustment layer to change an image's contrast—not Image > Adjustments > Levels/Curves.

ADJUSTMENT LAYERS

Add layer mask

You can also paint on the layer mask. Here, the contrast adjustment will only apply to the bottom of the image where the mask is painted white.

ADJUSTMENT LAYERS

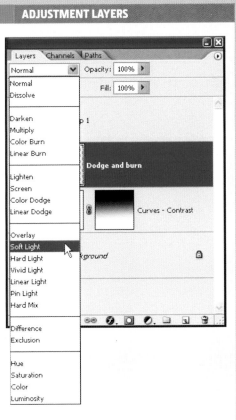

Every layer has a blending mode that controls how its pixel colors affect the underlying image.

LAYER GROUPS

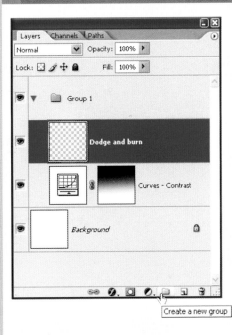

Create a new group

Layer groups or sets are a convenient way of applying a specific change to a number of different layers.

LAYER STYLES

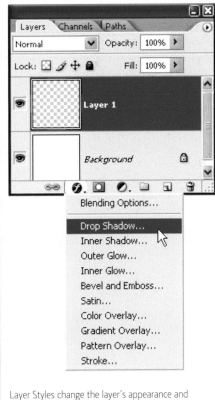

Blending Options...

Drop Shadow...
Inner Shadow...
Outer Glow...
Inner Glow...
Bevel and Emboss...
Satin...
Color Overlay...
Gradient Overlay...
Pattern Overlay...
Stroke...

Layer Styles change the layer's appearance and are completely non-destructive.

Using the selection tools

The work of imitating the styles of great painters, printmakers, and photographers requires extensive use of Photoshop's numerous selection tools. It's often necessary to isolate an image area before copying it to its own layer and applying a filter, stretching, or warping it; or when you need to extract an object and copy it to another image. The first step is almost always selection, and it's important to be able to switch fluidly between the various selection tools.

KEYBOARD SHORTCUTS

Shift	After you make a selection, holding down Shift lets you add to the selection
Alt/Opt	Subtracts pixels from an existing selection
Ctrl/Cmd + J	Copies the selection onto a new layer
Alt/Opt + Ctrl/Cmd + J	Copies the selection shows the new layer dialog box, letting you change the new layer's name, blending mode, and opacity
Ctrl/Cmd + Shift + J	Cuts out the selection and places it into a new layer
Ctrl/Cmd + Shift + I	Inverts or reverses the selection. This enables you to select an area that's easy to isolate (like a plain sky), then invert the selection to work on other parts of the image that would be difficult to select directly.

MARQUEE TOOLS

Rectangular Marquee Tool — M
Elliptical Marquee Tool — M
Single Row Marquee Tool
Single Column Marquee Tool

There are four Marquee tools, the most useful being Rectangular and Elliptical. These let you drag the cursor around the areas you want to select. If you hold down the Alt/Opt key, you can drag outward—I find this much more natural.

LASSO TOOLS

Lasso Tool — L
Polygonal Lasso Tool — L
Magnetic Lasso Tool — L

The Lasso tool allows you to create a selection in a more freehand manner. With the Polygonal Lasso, you click on several points, which are then joined up to form the selection. The Magic Lasso clings to the nearest edge, so you can move around an object and the tool will attempt to select it for you.

QUICK MASK SELECTION

Another powerful selection method is to enter Quick Mask mode (shortcut Q) and paint onto the mask. Paint black with the Brush tool and areas you paint will be visible as a mask overlay, usually the default pink-red. Black means the pixels are not selected, white means they are selected, and gray partially selects them. Vary the brush size and softness to suit the image features you wish to select, and zoom in on tricky areas. When you're ready, exit Quick Mask mode (Q) and you will see the selection's "marching ants." If you're still not happy with the selection, you can return to Quick Mask mode and paint either black or white to adjust the mask. This can be a very precise yet flexible way of working.

THE MAGIC WAND

The Magic Wand is useful for selecting a consistently colored area such as a blue sky. Click on a pixel and all the adjacent pixels that fall within a certain tolerance will be automatically selected.

Tolerance: 30 ☑ Anti-alias ☑ Contiguous ☐ Sample All Layers

COLOR RANGE

Color Range is similar to the Magic Wand, but is much more "visual," powerful, and flexible. First, use the Eyedropper tool to sample a color typical of the area you plan to select, then choose Select > Color Range. The resulting dialog box shows the selected pixels that match the sampled color. Use the Shift key and click other pixels on the image to add them to the selection, and use Alt/Opt to subtract them from the selection. Adjust the Fuzziness slider, too—generally the more colors you have sampled, the lower the Fuzziness needs to be. I also find it useful to switch the Selection Preview between the different options.

SOFTENING THE SELECTION'S EDGE

When you use tools such as the Marquee, Lasso, and Magic Wand to select an area, the selection's edges will often be rough. If you immediately apply a filter to the selected area, or move it to another image, the transition will be ugly and the edges will show. You need to soften the selection's edges.

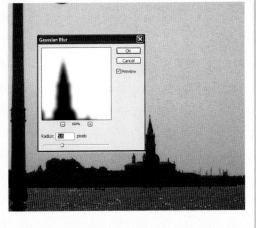

One way to soften the transition is Select > Feather. However, this is a rather crude method with the disadvantage of having no preview, so you have to guess at how many pixels to select. It's most successful when you've made a very precise selection of an object you want to cut out of a picture. In these cases, a feather radius of 1 or 2 can help the object fit in to its new background.

A better choice is to enter Quick Mask mode (Q), which enables you to preview the softening of the selection edge. The mask is usually a pink-red overlay, with the selected area being clear. Select Filter > Blur > Gaussian Blur and adjust the Radius slider. The mask's edge softens. When you feel its edge is soft enough, click OK, and exit Quick Mask by pressing Q again.

Fine-tuning colors

Look at many "Old Masters" and you will see the distinctive color cast of varnish and age, as well as the idiosyncrasies of the original oil paints. Similarly, early photographs are not black and white but many different shades—sepia, bright blue, purple, and so on. To help your picture hint at its inspiration, Photoshop offers numerous ways to fine-tune colors.

ENRICHING COLORS

Selective Color adjustment layers enable you to enrich certain colors without unbalancing others. I find them useful when I want to simulate the use of a polarizing filter. To beef up the sky, for example, I choose Blues from the Colors drop-down box, and drag the Black slider to the right.

BETTER BLACK AND WHITE

Many of the projects in the Photographers and Painters sections involve changing a color image to black and white, and they almost always include the use of a Channel Mixer adjustment layer with the Monochrome box checked. As I've said before, there is no single best way to do anything in Photoshop, but this method is the one I prefer. I do so because achieving a good black-and-white image takes much more than just removing the color—which immediately makes me rule out "quick-fix" methods such as Image > Mode > Grayscale and Image > Adjustments > Desaturate. Another approach uses Image > Mode > Lab Color, after which you delete the "a" channel—but this makes no allowances for fine-tuning the conversion to black and white and making the result more expressive.

Using the Channel Mixer adjustment layer method means you are mixing the black-and-white image using the information in the different RGB channels. This enables you to make subtle changes, such as emphasizing the sky by reducing the Red channel value (which will be low in a blue sky). You can also use multiple Channel Mixer adjustment layers with masks, giving you the ability to convert different image areas independently.

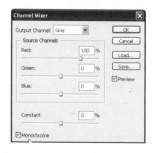

To make an image black and white, add a Channel Mixer adjustment layer and tick Monochrome. Then drag the sliders until the black-and-white image looks its best. I tend to adjust the sliders so that the three channels' values add up to 100%, and then adjust the brightness with another adjustment layer, if necessary.

COLOR SAMPLER

The Color Sampler lets you place markers in the image. Their RGB channel values are then displayed in the Info panel.

COLOR MATCHING

When you need to match an exact color, the Eyedropper tool lets you click within a picture and measure the tone. It also makes it into the foreground color.

Solid Color...
Gradient...
Pattern...

Levels...
Curves...
Color Balance...
Brightness/Contrast...

Hue/Saturation...
Selective Color...
Channel Mixer...
Gradient Map...
Photo Filter...

Invert
Threshold...
Posterize...

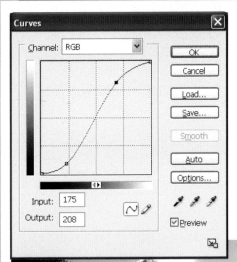

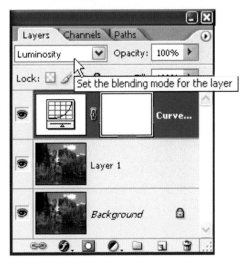

Set the blending mode for the layer

Eliminate the color shift by changing the Curves adjustment layer's blending mode to Luminosity.

Photo Filter

Use
- Filter: Warming Filter (85)
- Color:

Density: 50 %

☑ Preserve Luminosity

☑ Preview

Curves adjustment layers are great for changing image contrast. Click points on the curve and drag them, watching the way in which they affect the image. However, Curves can introduce unwanted color shifts, such as the cyan in the sky.

A Photo Filter adjustment layer is a quick way to warm up or cool down an image. They are designed to simulate the lens filters used by many photographers.

Hue/Saturation

Edit: Master

Hue: 198

Saturation: 25

Lightness: 0

☑ Colorize
☑ Preview

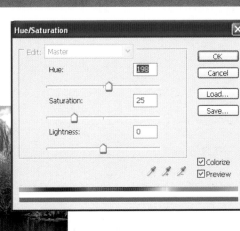

A quick way to give a picture a tone is to add a Hue/Saturation adjustment layer and tick Colorize. See pages 54–55 for a more sophisticated toning method.

27

Filters

You can apply a Photoshop filter to the active, visible layer of an image or to a selection, and its appearance will change, either subtly or dramatically. Almost every recipe in this book includes specific applications of filters, so here we'll take an overview and seek out some of their more under-utilized features.

First, be careful—filters change pixels. While the file is open, you can use History to step back to a stage before the application of a filter, but once you close the file, you lose the ability to reverse your changes. Apply filters to a copy of the image layer.

Notice that some filters work differently depending on Photoshop's foreground and background colors. For instance, the Pointillize filter uses the background color to fill in the gaps between the dots, while the Clouds filter uses both the foreground and background colors to create artificial clouds. If you don't want red or purple clouds, review the current colors before you apply the filter. Hit D to set the colors back to the default black and white.

It's common to preview a filter, fine-tune it, apply it—and immediately change your mind. Sure, you can use Undo or Ctrl/Cmd + Z to reverse the filter completely. But you might just want to partially undo its effects, and that's when Edit > Fade becomes handy. Shift + Ctrl/Cmd + F is the keyboard shortcut, but the command is only available until you do something else in Photoshop, after which it is grayed out. The Edit > Fade dialog also lets you access the blending mode Photoshop uses for calculating the partial Undo. So you could simply reduce the strength of a filter, but if you selected the Darken mode, it would retain the effect on those pixels where the filter had darkened the image.

If you like a filter and want to apply it on top of its first application, remember that Ctrl/Cmd + F runs the last filter that you applied with identical settings. Another option, Alt/Opt-Ctrl/Cmd + F, runs the filter but displays the dialog box.

You can also buy plug-ins for Photoshop—third-party programs that can produce specific image transformations. Some, like black-and-white converters, I simply don't trust, though their film grain features could be interesting, if somewhat misleading (process a film using the wrong developer or with different timings, and the film's grain will vary, too). Others simulate line engraving and other special effects and do look promising. Try them if you like, but I won't be covering them here. There's a lot of Photoshop to explore first!

28

USING FILTERS

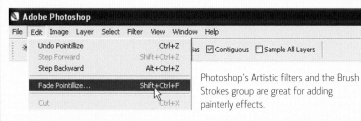

Photoshop's Artistic filters and the Brush Strokes group are great for adding painterly effects.

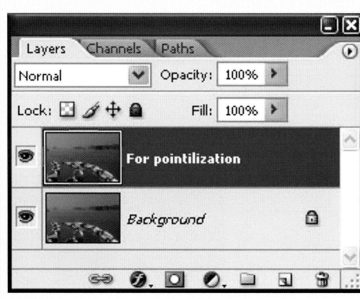

Apply filters to a copy of the image layer in case you don't like the effect and want to return to the original image.

This scene in Matsushima Bay in northern Japan struck me as the kind of subject Seurat would have liked.

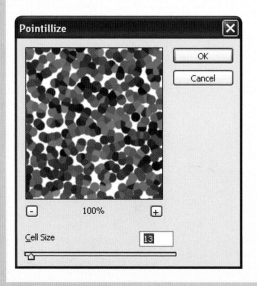

Most filter dialogs contain sliders that allow you to control the filter's effects. The arrow keys on the keyboard move sliders one unit at a time, but hold down Shift to move sliders 10 units.

Pointillize simulates a late-Impressionist painting style made famous by the French artist Georges Seurat.

Last Filter	Ctrl+F
Extract...	Alt+Ctrl+X
Filter Gallery...	
Liquify...	Shift+Ctrl+X
Pattern Maker...	Alt+Shift+Ctrl+X
Vanishing Point...	Alt+Ctrl+V
Artistic ▶	Colored Pencil...
Blur ▶	Cutout...
Brush Strokes ▶	Dry Brush...
Distort ▶	Film Grain...
Noise ▶	Fresco...
Pixelate ▶	Neon Glow...
Render ▶	Paint Daubs...
Sharpen ▶	Palette Knife...
Sketch ▶	Plastic Wrap...
Stylize ▶	Poster Edges...
Texture ▶	Rough Pastels...
Video ▶	Smudge Stick...
Other ▶	Sponge...
Digimarc ▶	Underpainting...
	Watercolor...

Immediately after you apply a filter, Edit > Fade is available. This allows you to fine-tune the effect of the filter.

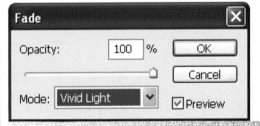

The Fade dialog can partially undo the effects of a filter.

Here I applied Edit > Fade but selected the Vivid Light blending mode, which increased the color contrast.

Making your own brushes and patterns

To add a really individual touch to a picture, try painting on it using one of Photoshop's textured brushes. This is one way to simulate a distinctive brushstroke style such as Van Gogh's. Alternatively, you may wish to prepare an image area before applying filters or making other changes.

Patterns are equally flexible. You can fill an image area with them, or you can use them in Layer Styles that remain fully editable.

BUILT-IN BRUSHES

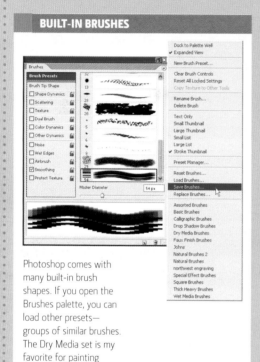

Photoshop comes with many built-in brush shapes. If you open the Brushes palette, you can load other presets—groups of similar brushes. The Dry Media set is my favorite for painting interesting textures onto a picture.

USING LAYERS

Whatever your experience of real-world painting, in the digital realm you should always paint onto a separate layer. Even when you are confident, you can still make mistakes.

You may want to try out a variation on your painting. Simply duplicate the painting layer and hide your initial attempt. You can always toggle the layers' visibility and decide which works best, or maintain many variations for different purposes.

MAKING A BRUSH

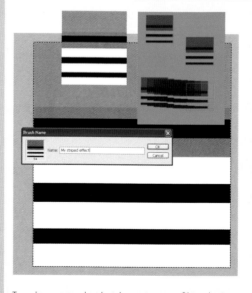

Once you have defined your custom brush, it's no different from any other and can be used to apply any color you choose.

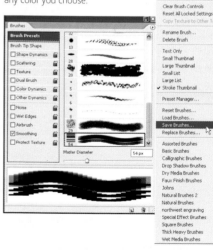

To make your own brush style, create a new file and paint pixels with shades of black, white, and gray. Black pixels will be like the brush hairs, where your Photoshop brush will apply paint; white is like the gaps between the hairs; and gray will apply paint with varying opacity. Here I used the Marquee to select blocks of pixels and Edit > Fill to color them. Save your brush definition with Edit > Define Brush.

Now and then, it's a good idea to save your brushes. The Brushes palette has a Save command that exports the palette's contents to an external file. You can back up this file, or use it on other computers.

MAKING A PATTERN

Defining a pattern is as easy as saving a brush definition. Here I selected a picture and saved it as a pattern.

FILLING AREAS WITH A PATTERN

One way to use your pattern is to select an area, then select Edit > Fill and choose Pattern from the Use drop-down box. As usual, use a new layer.

USING YOUR PATTERNS AS A LAYER STYLE

In this picture, I created a fog pattern and applied it to the whole layer as a Pattern Overlay, greatly increasing its size.

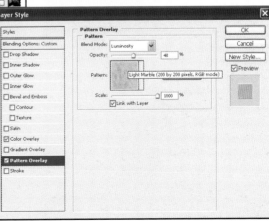

A more flexible way to apply your pattern is to click the "Add a layer style" icon in the Layers palette and select Pattern Overlay.

You can also apply your pattern in the Layer Style dialog box—and here, unlike Edit > Fill, you can vary its size. You can save your file, return to it later, and change the pattern's settings.

Making frames and borders

You wouldn't expect to see the Mona Lisa in a chrome frame—and would you believe it was the real thing if you did? Equally, a fine piece of photojournalism wouldn't hit so hard if the frame was decorated with gold leaf. When your photograph finally resembles its intended style, you might want to display it appropriately, too. That might mean looking around for the right frame, but you might also want a copy for your portfolio. One approach is to add a fake frame or decorative border to the picture.

Many of the recipes in the Photographers and Painters & Printmakers sections mention adding frames and borders as finishing touches. You can buy Photoshop plug-ins for making them, but it's easy enough to do it yourself. The same process of reflection, analysis, and improvisation applies. Let's try simulating a fancy frame with rounded corners.

Once you've created a digital frame, you can easily drag another picture into it.

YOU'VE BEEN FRAMED

1 Use Ctrl/Cmd + - (minus) to zoom out and give yourself a little screen room.

2 Increase the canvas size for your image. One way is to activate the Crop tool and select the entire image area—the canvas—and then hold down the Alt/Opt key and drag one corner outward. Double-click the image to apply the increased canvas size.

3 Select the Rounded Rectangle tool (it's in the same group as the Line tool).

4 Set the tool's Path option. Adjust its corner roundness and the Radius setting.

5 Drag the rectangle over the image.

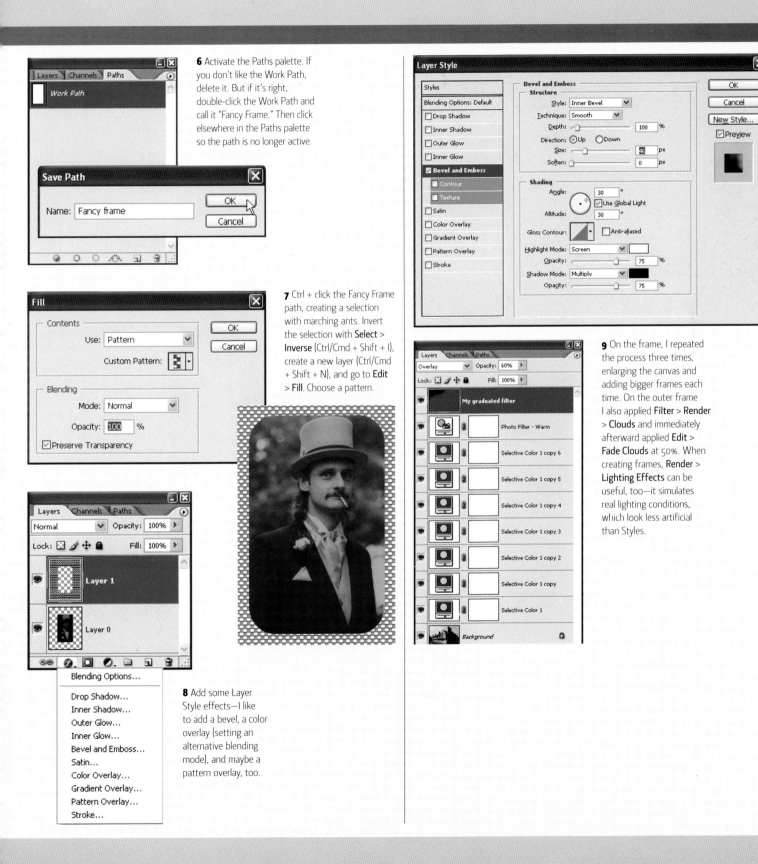

6 Activate the Paths palette. If you don't like the Work Path, delete it. But if it's right, double-click the Work Path and call it "Fancy Frame." Then click elsewhere in the Paths palette so the path is no longer active.

7 Ctrl + click the Fancy Frame path, creating a selection with marching ants. Invert the selection with **Select > Inverse** (Ctrl/Cmd + Shift + I), create a new layer (Ctrl/Cmd + Shift + N), and go to **Edit > Fill**. Choose a pattern.

8 Add some Layer Style effects—I like to add a bevel, a color overlay (setting an alternative blending mode), and maybe a pattern overlay, too.

9 On the frame, I repeated the process three times, enlarging the canvas and adding bigger frames each time. On the outer frame I also applied **Filter > Render > Clouds** and immediately afterward applied **Edit > Fade Clouds** at 50%. When creating frames, **Render > Lighting Effects** can be useful, too—it simulates real lighting conditions, which look less artificial than Styles.

PHOTOGRAPHERS

Creating images in the
styles of the world's
greatest photographers

Daguerreotypes

The world's first photographic process was announced in Paris in 1839 by Louis Daguerre. It used a silver-plated copper sheet that was sensitized with iodine, exposed, and then developed in mercury vapor. Early images were of architectural subjects or landscapes, but soon the process was also used for portraiture, and it became particularly popular in France and America. Daguerreotypes were positive images, one-offs, and the process was obsolete within a decade, as soon as new techniques allowed multiple photographs to be printed from negatives. But if you ever get the opportunity to compare early photographs in museums or exhibitions, it would be surprising if you didn't find the Daguerreotypes to be some of the most magical objects on display.

Early Daguerreotype exposure times were long, so moving subjects such as water and people usually appeared blurred. Photoshop's Motion Blur filter is ideal for simulating this, but requires a little care in its application because Daguerreotypes recorded other, static objects in fine detail. The other major characteristic of the Daguerreotype, its metal base, is tougher to imitate: the effect is as if the picture were printed onto a mirror. I didn't have any success using an inkjet printer to print onto kitchen foil, promising though this experiment seemed, but there are ways to imitate metallic finishes in Photoshop. Certainly you need to print onto high-gloss paper rather than a surface with a matte or textured finish. The staining and other discoloration around the picture edges can also be added artificially in Photoshop, but it's quicker and more realistic to scan real materials and use them as layers within the picture. Metallic objects will be most suitable for the Daguerreotype, but once you get the hang of this technique, you can apply it to all sorts of photographs.

Choose any image to which you can add an obvious touch of movement—one with a river is perfect. If you're starting with a color image, go to Image > Adjustments > Desaturate to remove the color while staying in RGB mode. This picture of Notre Dame in Paris seems appropriate, though of course the couple would have moved during the long Daguerreotype exposure time. I exercised artistic license and left them static. The subjects of original studio portraits were strapped into chairs to keep them from moving, so this is not so improbable!

I used a steel picture frame, scanned on a flatbed scanner, to simulate the Daguerreotype's silver-coated plate.

1 With your picture file open, identify a feature of the photograph that might move during a long exposure, and select it. Here I selected the river by clicking with the Magic Wand along the water's edge. To make any edges between blurred and static areas less visible, feather the selection using **Select > Feather** and a radius of 1 or 2 pixels.

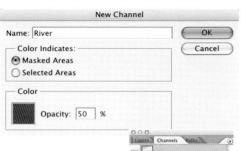

2 Saving selections adds to the file size but saves you lots of time if you need to reselect an object later. Save your selection in the Layers palette by holding down the Alt/Opt key as you click the "Save selection as channel" icon, and give this alpha channel a name that's easy to recognize.

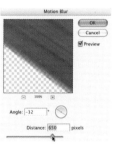

3 To convey the impression of movement, copy the selected feature into its own layer using Ctrl/Cmd + J, and then select **Filter > Blur > Motion Blur**. You can judge the angle of movement by eye, but I prefer to use the Measure tool. Here I used the tool along the nearside riverbank, read the angle indication in the Info palette, and entered the angle in the Motion Blur filter dialog. You also need to set a very high Distance value to mimic the flow of the water during a long exposure. You'll need to repeat this process of selecting and blurring for each "moving" object.

4 Open the file with the metallic plate texture, and drag and drop the image from the Layers palette onto the main image. In the Layers palette, change its blending mode to Multiply and adjust the layer's opacity. Multiply lets both the picture and the texture layer show through—feel free to experiment with other blending modes, and also with placing the texture above or below the image in the layer stack. Use **Edit > Free Transform** to resize and position the texture.

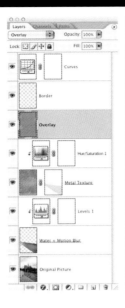

5 With a real Daguerreotype, the edges are unevenly stained with vivid blue and orange chemical colors. Imitate this on a separate layer. Hold down the Alt/Opt key, and click the "Create a new layer" icon in the Layers palette. In the Mode drop-down box, select Overlay and click OK.

6 Load a soft-edged brush from Photoshop's Dry Media Brushes, set the opacity to about 30%, and then paint roughly around the layer. The colors can vary; here, I preferred more subdued tones.

7 Any image is likely to need some fine-tuning after these key steps. I added a Levels adjustment layer to brighten the water layer, and reduced the metal texture's blue color by adding a Hue/Saturation layer. In each case, you can prevent an adjustment layer affecting all layers by "grouping" it with the target layer—hold down the Alt/Opt key and click the line between the two layers. I also reused my River selection to paint on various layer masks. The finishing touches were a Curves adjustment layer to brighten the overall image, and a white border—this was a rectangular selection, the corners of which were rounded using **Select > Modify > Smooth**.

Early Daguerreotypes were highly polished, very delicate, and easily scratched, and the chemical processes were not yet fixed and dependable. Yet they remain the most beautiful of the early photographs.

Calotypes and salted paper prints

While Louis Daguerre was the first to announce his technique, in the 1830s, the English scientist Henry Fox Talbot had also been working on a photographic process. The Calotype was a negative-positive method that permitted multiple prints of the same image. The negative was prepared by impregnating paper with light-sensitive chemicals, and then drying, exposing, and developing it to create a "paper negative." The print was usually made by contact printing—the negative and a sheet of similarly sensitized "salted paper" were sandwiched together under a piece of glass and exposed to bright sunlight. In France, the process was developed further with Gustave Le Gray's "waxed paper" process, which produced much finer detail, but Fox Talbot's patents and licensing fees limited its commercial appeal. Calotype negatives were rapidly superseded in the 1850s by the wet-plate collodion process.

Before coining the word "Calotype," Fox Talbot's early works involved placing leaves, lace, and other objects directly onto salted paper. No camera was involved in these "photogenic drawings." So, taking the idea of scanning real material one step further, you can do something similar using a flatbed scanner to capture objects such as the kiwi fruit in this recipe.

You will probably need to extract the objects from their background. Find some paper that has gentle fibers and scan that, too—this can be combined with the subject to imitate the paper negative's typical softness. A third quality, the sepia tone, is easy enough to create in Photoshop.

A thin slice of kiwi fruit and some bathroom tissue were scanned separately with an ordinary flatbed scanner. Be sure that you know how to clean the scanner glass properly so that any juice or liquid will not leave a mark.

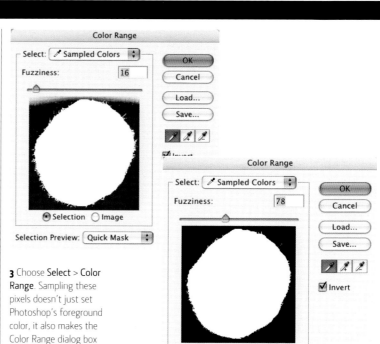

1 If your subject is predominantly white—a piece of lace, for example—place it on the scanner with a plain, brightly colored card as a background. This will make it easier for you to isolate the item from the bcakground. Scan the item and then make a separate scan of the paper you've selected to use to add texture to the final image. Leave the windows of both scans open in Photoshop.

2 Like the uneven gray-blue tone around my kiwi, your scan will probably capture some of the scanner's white lid or the colored sheet. To remove these areas, select the Eyedropper tool and click in one of those areas to sample the color. I sampled a pixel color that was somewhere between the darkest and the lightest gray-blue shade.

3 Choose **Select > Color Range**. Sampling these pixels doesn't just set Photoshop's foreground color, it also makes the Color Range dialog box assume you want to select pixels matching the sampled color, and immediately selects those pixels. Check the Invert checkbox so that the fruit or other object is shown in white, meaning it will be selected, and adjust the Fuzziness slider until all the unwanted pixels show as black in the preview. Click OK.

4 With the selection's marching ants active, check the Layers palette. If the image is shown as a locked background layer (with its name displayed in italics), double-click the thumbnail and rename the layer. This enables the layer to have transparent pixels.

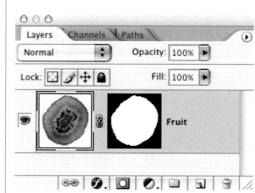

5 Click the "Add layer mask" icon. The unwanted pixels are hidden, or "masked." This technique is more flexible than simply deleting the pixels because it allows you to fine-tune the subject's edges, or redo the extraction entirely. Flexibility is also why I used Color Range rather than the Magic Wand, **Filter > Extract**, or the other selection tools.

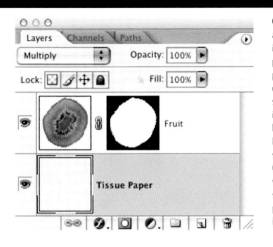

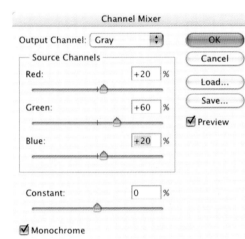

6 To combine the subject and the paper scan, drag the image layer from the Layers palette and drop it into the paper scan's window. Hold down the Shift key as you do so to automatically center the image. Change the image layer's blending mode to Multiply and the paper will show through (mimicking Calotype images, which were absorbed into the salted paper, unlike modern photographs where the image is usually a plastic coating).

7 Add a Channel Mixer adjustment layer (see page 26) to make the picture monochrome. Early photographic processes had greater sensitivity to blue light, which made skies appear lighter and skin tones darker. To mimic this, use higher Blue channel values and lower Red channel values (don't treat this as gospel, though—if other values look better for your particular image, go with them).

8 To add the sepia tone typical of a Calotype, create a Hue/Saturation adjustment layer, tick the Colorize checkbox and set Hue to 30 and Saturation to 20. The Hue value may be lower or higher—the color of the Calotype varied between a reddish-brown and a yellowish tone. The colors were always subdued, so keep the saturation low. If you need to adjust the picture's contrast, add a Curves layer, but always aim for a low-contrast final result.

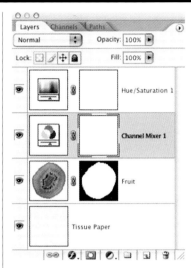

9 Finally, salted paper prints did not have a glossy finish, so try to print your pseudo-Calotype onto matte paper. If the print has any borders, cut them right back with a guillotine or art knife so that the sepia tone extends to the paper's edge. For extra authenticity, you could cut little triangles off the corners, and then mount the print directly onto a card.

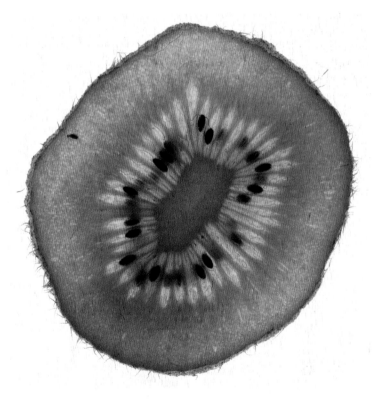

Fox Talbot's earliest images were made without a camera by placing objects directly onto light-sensitive paper. You can use a flatbed scanner to capture both the subject and its textured surface.

Cartes de visite

Postcard-sized cartes de visite depicted the personalities of the day and were popular collectibles in the mid-19th century. One of the most celebrated collections belonged to John Hay, President Abraham Lincoln's personal secretary. Hay knew cartes de visite photographers such as Matthew Brady and Alexander Gardner, who held stocks of autographed cartes, and like many collectors, he sent cartes to subjects with requests that they be returned with signatures.

There are two main steps to creating a Photoshop carte de visite. First, make a template for your standard carte. It could have a decorative border, and, for added authenticity, some printed text to advertise your "studio." Secondly, add the photograph as a vignette and include a handwritten signature, and then finish it with some sepia toning and any other details specific to the subject. This isn't at all difficult to master, and you can easily produce a collection of cartes featuring friends or family members.

When you're applying aging effects to an image, it always helps if the picture has a suitably "vintage" look to begin with. Battle reconstructions and other historical reenactments can be a useful source of such material.

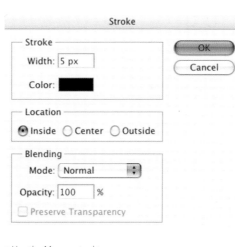

1 Create a new document. Set the resolution to 300ppi and enter the size—typically, cartes were around 2 x 4in (5 x 10cm). Set Background Contents to White.

2 Use the Marquee tool to select a rectangle close to the edge of the image, and use **Edit > Stroke** to add a 5-pixel black line.

3 Making sure you still have the selection's marching ants visible, contract it a little and add another, thinner line. Use **Select > Modify > Contract** and enter 10, then add another 2-pixel black line with **Edit > Stroke**.

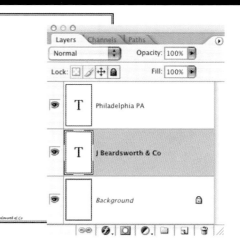

4 Next, add some printed text near the base of the image. Activate the Text tool, choose a font that has an authentic period "feel," and add your name and a city—19th-century photographers often used cartes to promote their studios. This completes the standard carte. Save the file before you proceed.

5 Open the file with the subject's photograph, desaturate it with **Image > Adjustments > Desaturate**, and then drag the image layer into the carte de visite window. If it's too big, use **Edit > Transform** to resize and position it, holding down the Shift key as you drag the corner handles only. Don't fill the frame—cartes often used relatively small images. When you're done, hit the Enter key or double-click the transformation box.

40

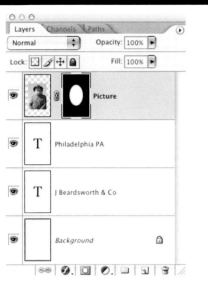

6 Use the Elliptical Marquee tool to select the area you want to show in the vignette window. When you are satisfied, click the "Add layer mask" icon in the Layers palette.

7 To create the vignette's soft edge, click on the right, monochrome thumbnail in the Layers palette to make sure that the mask icon is active, rather than the photo icon, so the mask can be blurred. Choose **Filter** > **Blur** > **Gaussian Blur** and drag the slider until the picture's edge is soft, and click OK. Vignettes were originally created by hand, which you can do, too, using a soft brush to paint on the mask—white reveals the image, black hides it.

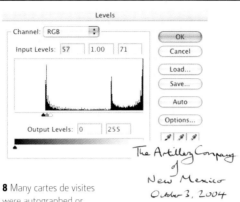

8 Many cartes de visites were autographed or annotated by hand. To mimic this, write your text in a dark color on plain white paper, scan it with a flatbed scanner, and open the image in Photoshop. Click on the new file to make it active, but ensure you can still see the carte's window. Drag the new file from the Layers palette and drop it into the carte image—it will become a new layer. Resize as necessary, then change the layer's blending mode to Darken. If necessary, use **Image** > **Adjustments** > **Levels** to convert the writing to pure black and white. Do this by dragging the shadows and highlights sliders in from either end, around the spike representing the text.

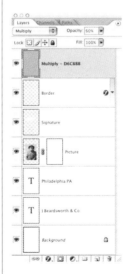

9 Finally, you need to adjust the colors so that they have a faded, sepia tone. Add a new layer and change its blending mode to Multiply. Then set the foreground color to a sepia (try RGB values of 214, 203, 187), and fill the layer with color using **Edit** > **Fill**. You can also vary the layer's opacity if you want to moderate the tone.

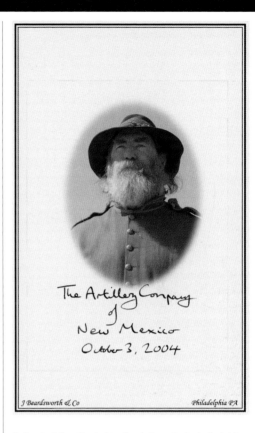

Cartes de visites often feature the photographer's studio details, autographs, and other handwritten notes.

Cartes de visites were popular collectibles in the mid-19th century and were often displayed in albums. I deliberately left some printed text visible, and placed one image slightly off-center.

41

Ambrotypes and tintypes

While researching wet-plate collodion methods, Frederick Scott Archer found that by placing an underexposed glass negative in front of a dark background, he could produce a positive image. This was the ambrotype or collodion positive, which was a more economical process than the Daguerreotype, and produced sharper, clearer images than Fox Talbot's paper negatives. The tintype (or ferrotype) used a metal rather than glass negative and was an even cheaper variation. Tintypes were robust enough to be sent by mail, or could be cut and mounted in lockets, and they were especially popular in the late 19th century as they enabled photographers to offer small, near-instant pictures to a much wider cross-section of society.

As always, it is worthwhile examining examples of ambrotypes and tintypes in museums, books, or online. Typically, the subject matter would be a portrait, and, because cheap tintypes could be made by street or traveling photographers, the subjects were often ordinary folks rather than more affluent citizens. An important characteristic is that ambrotypes and tintypes are laterally reversed—important if a picture included lettering or distinctive patterns. With sepia-toned ambrotypes and tintypes, the toning is usually subdued. They both tend to contain dark grays rather than blacks, and ambrotypes appear to lack whites—perhaps not surprising, as they have dark backgrounds. Both types of pictures were sometimes hand-colored, usually without much subtlety.

42

This black-and-white picture was taken at a wedding in the north of England, but I liked its Old West feel. The tintype in particular was hugely popular in the United States.

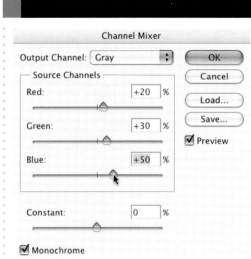

1 If you are starting with a color picture, convert it to black and white using Image > Adjustments > Channel Mixer. Check the Monochrome option. Increase the value of the Blue channel more than the others, but try to ensure that the overall sum of the Red, Green, and Blue channel adjustments is around 100%. Aim for a low-contrast image.

2 In the Layers palette, click the "Create a new fill or adjustment layer" icon. Select Levels. In the resulting dialog box, drag the two Output sliders at the very bottom of the dialog inward, so the picture's darkest black will be a deep gray and whites will be very dark.

CURVES

As an alternative to step two's Levels, you could use Curves. By dragging the curve's bottom left hand corner up, and its top right down, the same effect is created, but you are still able to add points for more precise tonal control.

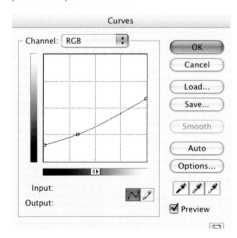

3 To add a sepia tone, click the "Create a new fill or adjustment layer" icon and select Hue/Saturation. Check the Colorize box, and drag the Hue slider to about 30 and the Saturation to a low value of around 10.

4 For each item that you want to color, hold down the Alt/Opt key and click the "Create a new layer" icon. Give it a memorable name and change the layer's blending mode to Color. Choosing this mode means you can paint on the layer and the underlying picture will show through.

New Layer

Name: Cravat
☐ Use Previous Layer to Create Clipping Mask
Color: ☐ None
Mode: Color   Opacity: 100 %
☐ (No neutral color exists for Color mode.)

OK
Cancel

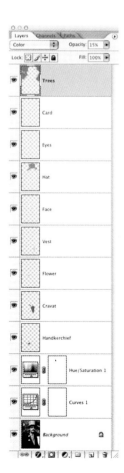

5 Select a brush and paint onto the layer. For small areas, zoom right in, change the brush size with the [and] keys, and soften the edges of the brush using Shift. If you paint too many pixels, you can use Undo, the Eraser tool, and the History Brush. But don't forget you are copying a manual process, the results of which were variable.

6 Some Photoshop users would paint all the different colors onto one layer, but there are many reasons why it's better to use a different layer for each colored area. They all amount to flexibility. In general, I deliberately paint with strong colors and then tone them down. Even if you paint separate objects identically, as I did with the cravat and handkerchief, if each has its own layer, you can reduce the layer's opacity on its own and not alter the others. If necessary, you can discard or duplicate and try alternative colors.

Ambrotypes are underexposed glass negatives on a black background and can often be very dark. Tintypes tend to be brighter, but are generally smaller and cheaper-looking. Both types of images were often presented in very elaborate frames. This is the frame made on page 32.

Wet-plate collodion

Wet-plate collodion was the primary photographic process in use between the 1850s and 1880s. Collodion was a viscous liquid used to coat glass plates with light-sensitive salts, which needed to be wet when the picture was exposed. The glass negatives were contact-printed onto albumen-impregnated paper that was often toned with gold chloride, which imbued a purplish-brown color. The subject matter was very wide—Matthew Brady, Alexander Gardner, and Timothy O'Sullivan depicted the American Civil War and the Gold Rush, while British photographers such as Roger Fenton and Francis Frith celebrated the Empire and its engineering achievements. As the technology improved, shorter exposure times and better optics enabled photographers to capture such scenes with unprecedented realism.

If you're starting with a color image, you can convert it to black and white to replicate the subdued quality and the pale, featureless skies typical of pictures made with the wet-plate collodion process. The toning needs to be simulated, and, given that the original photographs are now 150 years old, aging and distressing the image would also be appropriate.

This photograph was taken with a zoom lens and has a modern, close-cropped composition, but the subject matter is appropriate to the period. American Civil War enthusiasts, such as the subjects of this picture, go to great lengths to recreate the past, but often don't have good pictures of themselves in period dress. You may be presented with great photographic opportunities if you approach them directly and offer copies of your pictures.

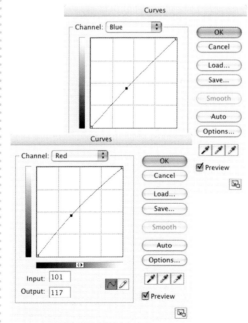

1 Open your photograph and convert it to black and white by clicking the "Create new fill or adjustment layer" icon and selecting Channel Mixer. Check the Monochrome checkbox and adjust the sliders until you achieve the desired result. For wet-plate collodion effects, you should use more of the Blue channel and less of the Red; this will lighten blues and keep skin tones subdued.

2 Next, add the tone. Click the "Create new fill or adjustment layer" icon and choose Curves. From the Channel drop-down menu, select the Red and Blue channels, and drag their curves slightly upward until you have a sepia-purple tone. This needs to be subtle, so be cautious with the effect.

3 Open the image containing the texture you want to use to degrade the photograph. This may be something you have created in Photoshop—but what could be easier than using real materials? Here, I used my flatbed scanner to import a torn, folded manila envelope—perfect for distressing the photograph.

4 In the texture image's Layers palette, pick up the image layer (by clicking and holding with the mouse) and drag it into the main photograph's window. Change the resulting layer's blending mode to Multiply.

Other modes, such as Hard Light and Pin Light, can also work, but they have strong effects and it's more important at this point to decide whether the texture is suitable. You can always try them later.

44

5 If the texture looks right, use **Edit > Transform** or Ctrl/Cmd + T to resize and position it. Drag the handles at each side of the transformation box. When you're done, double-click inside the box or hit the Enter key. Check that the texture doesn't become too obvious once it is magnified—you may need to scan a larger piece of material, or re-scan at a higher resolution.

6 The collodion mixture was hand-coated onto the glass plates and was often uneven. One way to simulate this is to select the picture layer, click the "Add layer mask" icon, apply the Clouds filter to the mask, and then immediately use **Edit > Fade Clouds** to moderate the resulting blotchiness.

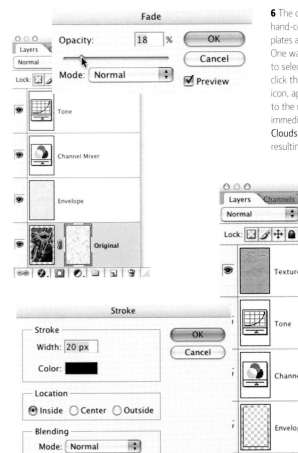

The aging effects have produced a result that suspends disbelief enough for us to overlook the high quality of the lens and the close crop.

7 Other finishing touches include adding a rough border on a separate layer, and fine-tuning the toning. You can also increase the Canvas Size and stretch the texture layer to fit—in this case, the folds of the paper show outside the image border, adding authenticity.

Cyanotypes

The first book of photographs was produced in 1843 by Anna Atkins, who used the cyanotype process discovered by scientist Sir John Herschel (who coined the word "photography"). Atkins placed ferns and other translucent plants on top of paper impregnated with iron-salt and exposed them to sunlight for around 15 minutes, or until an image had formed. The paper was then washed, leaving a fine negative "photogram" on a vivid blue background. The cyanotype was one of the few early techniques to continue into the 20th century, and was also used for architectural drawings, or "blueprints." It remains the most accessible alternative process because you don't need a darkroom and the chemicals are available from specialist suppliers. Some enthusiasts make photograms in the original style; others create negatives on their computers and print them onto acetate or paper made transparent with cooking oil, beeswax, or paraffin. These enlarged negatives are used to contact-print and make positive cyanotypes.

A cyanotype is instantly recognizable by the color that gave the process its name. The pictures tend to be low contrast and often have rough edges. Some earlier examples, such as calotypes (see page 38), have paper grain, but the process was used over such a long period that the physical condition and subject matter varies widely. If you can, print on matte, textured paper, as the photosensitive chemicals made cyanotype images part of the paper.

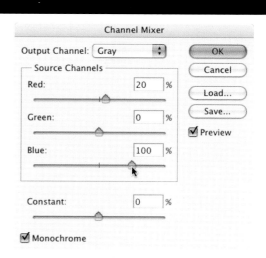

This old cemetery had fallen into disrepair and was heavily overgrown, making the crooked gravestone an appropriate and interesting subject.

1 If your original picture is in color, make it black and white using a Channel Mixer adjustment layer (see page 26). In general, favor the Blue channel and aim for a low-contrast image.

2 In the Layers palette, add a Curves adjustment layer and select Blue from the Channel drop-down menu. Drag the Blue channel's curve upward, but don't close the dialog box.

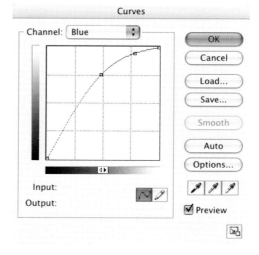

3 Select the Red channel and drag its curve downward. Adjust the Red and Blue channels until you achieve a cyan tone that you like. Cyanotypes vary between cyans and true blues to Prussian blues and the slight violet hue of some of Atkins's pictures.

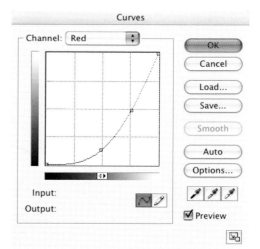

NEGATIVE EFFECT

To imitate a cyanotype photogram, you can scan objects and make them into negatives using an Invert Adjustment layer. This is the kiwi fruit that illustrated the calotype recipe. I also added a label—Atkins's pictures were scientific records.

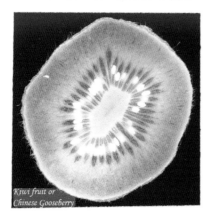

Kiwi fruit or Chinese Gooseberry

46

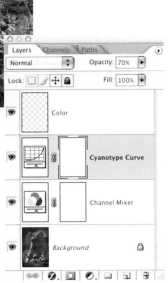

4 Cyanotypes were relatively stable, though some show discoloration, probably from adhesives. To emulate this, add a new layer and change its blending mode to Color; then select the Brush tool and paint onto the transparent pixels. If you want to simulate chemical staining, use a yellow color.

This is a 21st-century digital photograph of a 19th-century graveyard, made to look like a cyanotype. If you like this recipe, you may even want to experiment with the original process.

5 Another option is to add a rough border. Enlarge the canvas by clicking **Image > Canvas Size** and adding an appropriate distance to each axis (before you do, check that the Anchor square is in the center with an arrow pointing out on all sides—if not, click in the middle box).

Add a new layer and paint around its edges. A quick way to do this is to select the Brush tool and click one corner of the picture, which paints a dot. Then hold down the Shift key and click the next corner, and

Photoshop will paint between the two. In this example I loaded one of Photoshop's Dry Media set of brushes—they are nicely uneven and easily achieve the coated paper effect.

Stop-motion photography

In the 1870s, Leland Stanford, a former Governor of California, had Eadweard Muybridge photograph trotting and galloping horses to ascertain whether all four hooves were ever simultaneously off the ground (they were). Muybridge deployed banks of 12—and later 24—cameras, and used tripwires to release their shutters. Later studies depicted other moving animals and people, and were used by the French scientist Etienne-Jules Marey in his "zoetrope" drum, which rotated and conveyed lifelike movement. In fact, Marey's theories on animal movement had originally inspired Stanford's experiment.

The key to imitating Muybridge's stop-motion style is to shoot a sequence of pictures of a moving subject. Digital video cameras often include the facility to extract frames into JPEG or TIFF format, and some digital still cameras have built-in video capabilities. You will probably get better quality shooting a series of pictures with a still camera. In either case, it's then a matter of methodically positioning them in Photoshop.

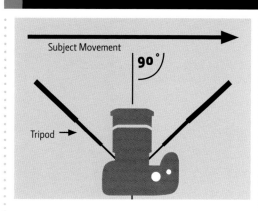

1 Mount the camera on a tripod at a right angle to the subject's path. Frame the scene with plenty of space at the sides, above, and in front. To ensure that every frame is identically composed, do not adjust the zoom or pan the camera. Focus on the subject and set the camera's focus mode to manual. Set a small aperture to keep the subject sharp if it moves a little toward or away from the camera. I also like to set the camera's exposure manually and wait for a moment when the lighting is constant.

2 From now on, all you need to do is release the shutter. If your camera can shoot rapid bursts of pictures, just ask the subject to move and fire away. Alternatively, shoot each frame individually, and then move the subject. Shoot as many frames as you need to capture the movement and to give you plenty of choices. In my series, inspired by a Muybridge shot of a woman stepping over a chair, I thought that eight frames worked well, and I asked each of the subjects to repeat the movement three times.

3 Open the best images in Photoshop, but don't adjust or crop them yet. Activate a picture in the sequence, hold down the Shift key, and drag the thumbnail from the Layers palette and drop it into the first picture's window. The Shift key makes sure the image is centered. Repeat the process for each shot, so they end up stacked in sequence in one document. If your computer is short on memory, you may have to keep open just the first picture and then open each subsequent file, drag and drop its picture, and close it again.

4 We need to crop the combined image, but to allow for the movement, it's useful to turn off the visibility of all the image layers except the top (last frame) and the last (first frame), and set the top layer's opacity to 50%. Use the Crop tool to select the area, double-click inside the selection box to apply the crop, and restore the last layer's opacity to 100%.

MATH

Paper width (19 inches)

x

Resolution (300 ppi)

=

Pixel width of page (5700)

÷

Number of pictures (8)

=

Width of one frame (712.5 pixels)

5 We need to resize the images so that they're smaller. This is a simple calculation. Multiply the paper size by the printing resolution (usually 300 ppi) to get the total paper size in pixels, and then divide by the number of frames—in this case eight. Round down the result and record it—I noted down 700 pixels. Then choose **Image > Resize** and enter the final picture size. I used 675 pixels because I allowed for a margin round each picture.

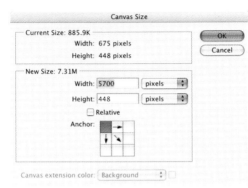

Canvas Size

Current Size: 885.9K
Width: 675 pixels
Height: 448 pixels

New Size: 7.31M
Width: 5700 pixels
Height: 448 pixels
☐ Relative
Anchor:

Canvas extension color: Background

Offset

Horizontal: 700 pixels right
Vertical: 0 pixels down
☑ Preview

Undefined Areas
⦿ Set to Transparent
○ Repeat Edge Pixels
○ Wrap Around

6 To make the Photoshop document large enough for the final layout, unlock the background layer by double-clicking on it and naming it Layer 0. Now use **Image > Canvas Size**, click the top-left Anchor square, enter the total paper width in pixels that you calculated in step 5 (see the box), and click OK.

7 Photoshop's Offset filter makes positioning layers easy and consistent. Activate Layer 1 in the Layers palette and choose **Filter > Other > Offset**, enter the space per pixel, and click OK. In this case I used 700 pixel measurement that I noted down at step 5. Then activate Layer 2 and press Ctrl/Cmd + F twice. For Layer 3, press Ctrl/Cmd + F three times and continue until all images are correctly positioned.

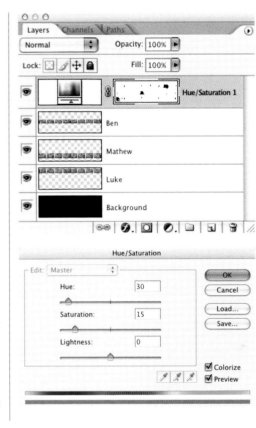

8 Here I have created two more rows of images for two more boys, but you could choose any number you like. To merge everything into one file, first flatten each sequence using **Layers > Flatten Image**. Then create a new file of appropriate width and height—in this case 5700 x 3900 pixels—and drag each flattened sequence into it as you did with the individual frames. Adjust their positions using the method from step 7. Finally, I added the sepia tone with a Hue/Saturation adjustment layer and carefully masked it in the same way as I used for ambrotypes and tintypes (see page 42).

49

There's no need to stop at a single, large print. You might take small prints of the original pictures and make a flipbook, or use them with other programs and make a slideshow or a QuickTime or Flash movie. After all, the true motion picture was only a short step beyond Muybridge's work.

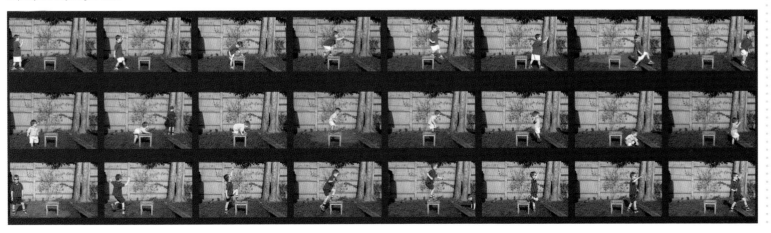

High art and the Pre-Raphaelites

While scientific experimentation drove much of photography's early history, other practitioners sought to marry its techniques to artistic interpretation and tradition. Julia Margaret Cameron aimed to "ennoble" photography, while Henry Peach Robinson wrote of "elevating the un-picturesque," and his writings gave the Pictorialists their name. Photographs often alluded to classical themes, while some of Robinson's most famous "combination prints" used multiple negatives to construct scenes that echoed the Pre-Raphaelite style and referred to contemporary poetry.

One element that becomes apparent upon examination of these High Art or Pre-Raphaelite photographs is the proliferation of circles and round-edged rectangles in their composition. Pay attention also to the tone—it is mainly a purple or red-brown that is characteristic of the late 19th-century albumen print. This name comes from the egg white used to bond the photographic emulsion to the paper. A quality typical of this paper type is its glazed finish—so make sure you print on glossy paper.

My "combination print" included a fruit bowl and two statues, and a scanned sheet of art paper.

1 Open the image which will serve as the background for your composition—in this case, the fruit bowl. Then open the other images and remove them from their backgrounds.

For this statue, choose **Filter > Extract** and use the Edge Highlighter tool to draw along the statue's edge, so the highlight covers both the subject and the background.

2 Once the edges are selected, select the Fill tool and click inside the highlighted area to indicate that you wish to keep the statue. Click OK,

review the accuracy of the extraction, and drag the image layer into the main background image. Repeat this for the other objects.

3 Position the various components using **Edit > Free Transform**. This enables you to move items and resize them. Hold down the Shift key to maintain the proportions of the object. Double-click inside the Transform box when you want to apply the changes.

4 Reposition the Eros statue behind the fruit bowl. Click the "Add layer mask" icon in the Layers palette and use a

soft brush to carefully paint black onto the mask, hiding the base of the statue.

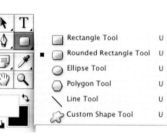

5 Before finalizing the combination of images, decide what shape you want your picture to be. Circles and arch shapes were favorites

among the Pre-Raphaelites. In order to create an arch shape, select the Rounded Rectangle tool (usually hidden behind the Rectangle tool).

6 In the Rounded Rectangle's Tool Options bar, make sure Shape layers are active; set a high radius to produce very rounded corners. Be sure that the foreground color is set to white, then click and drag from the top corner of the image to the bottom corner, continuing below

the image—the bottom corners of the rectangle will be outside the image area.

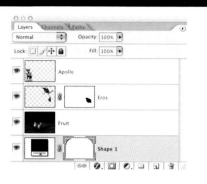

7 In the Layers palette, move the Shapes layer to the bottom of the layer stack.

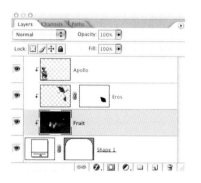

8 Holding down the Alt/Opt key, click the line in the Layers palette between the Shape layer and the next layer up, and repeat the process for each layer. The images now appear to be inside the arched shape, which serves as a clipping mask.

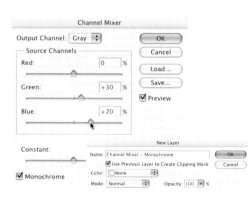

9 To make the image elements black and white, activate the top layer, then hold down the Alt/Opt key and click the Layers palette's "Create new fill or adjustment layer" icon.

Select Channel Mixer. Notice that "Use Previous layer to create Clipping Mask" is checked. In the Channel Mixer dialog box, check Monochrome and adjust the channel sliders.

10 To add a realistic selenium tone, add another adjustment layer, selecting Curves. Choose the Red channel, click a point near the curve's bottom left and drag it upward, then drag two more points so that the remainder of the curve is a relatively straight line as it moves through the midtones and highlights. Then choose the Blue channel, and drag its curve slightly upward—the tone can be anything from purple to red-brown.

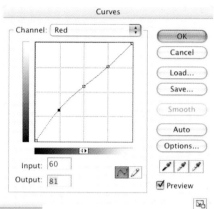

11 The final step is to add the scanned paper texture. Open the texture scan and drag it onto the main image. Move the Paper layer to the base of the layer stack. Notice how its color shows against the toned monochrome of the rest of the image. Finally, if you want the paper to show through the image, just change the Shape layer's blending mode to Multiply and lower its opacity.

"Music is the fruit of love." The High Art and Pre-Raphaelite photographers drew inspiration from their artistic heritage.

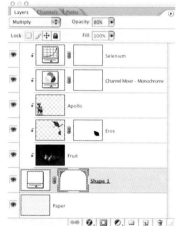

51

The Naturalists

Toward the end of the 19th century, Pictorialism and High Art had run their course, and contrived studio scenes and combination printing techniques were considered passé. In both America and Great Britain, exponents of the Naturalist approach sought a return to the fundamentals of photography. Naturalism's zealous British advocate, Peter Henry Emerson, attacked all artificiality and retouching; in America, Stieglitz and other leading Photo-Secessionists presented their work unapologetically as an art in its own right. The photograph still aimed to be a thing of beauty, but evolved into a record of everyday working-class life, often exposing the genuine hardship of its subjects. While some of the images taken by leading exponents such as Emerson and Sutcliff may have been more carefully contrived than the images themselves might suggest, they are interesting—and, indeed, radical—for representing the lives of ordinary working people, perhaps for the first time in the history of photography.

Emulating the style of Naturalism is less a question of digital manipulation than of careful choice of subject matter. Everyday scenes were captured in outdoor settings. Subjects appeared to be unaware of the photographer as they set to work in the fields or on fishing boats, and were often featured facing away from the camera. Look for water in the foreground, as featured in Emerson's photographs of Norfolk marshlands or Frank Sutcliff's harbour at Whitby in Yorkshire. Elements such as mist and smoke soften the picture. Echoing the ideas of the Impressionists, Emerson made use of natural, out-of-focus edges, and some of George Davison's most famous photographs have a remarkably diffuse quality. So be careful that you don't overwork the image—keep it soft and understated.

I selected this picture because water and reeds feature in many of Peter Emerson's wetland scenes.

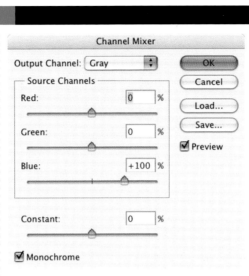

1 Panchromatic film—film sensitive to all colors of light—wasn't introduced until the 1910s, and until then, blue sky tended to look very light and clouds weakly defined. So, convert your image to black and white using higher Blue channel values—notice how the Red channel produces strong skies. In the Layers palette, click the "Create new fill or new adjustment layer" icon, select Channel Mixer, check Monochrome and drag the Blue slider up to 100% and the Red slider down to 0%.

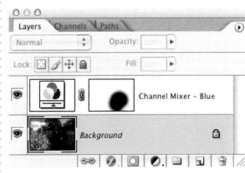

2 Always examine grayscale conversions carefully. You can often make a better black-and-white picture by converting distinct image areas individually. In this case, the Blue channel conversion makes the foreground water very dark, but see how the Red channel contains shadow detail in that area. To restrict the conversion, select the Brush tool (B), making sure it is soft-edged so that any transitions will be smooth, and set Foreground Color to Black (D). Click the adjustment layer mask in the Layers palette and paint away the conversion in the affected area.

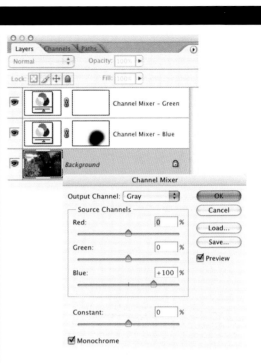

3 Add another Channel Mixer adjustment layer and adjust the sliders to fine-tune the conversion. Use the Green channel to convert the remaining colored areas. You will seldom require more than one extra conversion layer, but there is no reason why you shouldn't use more.

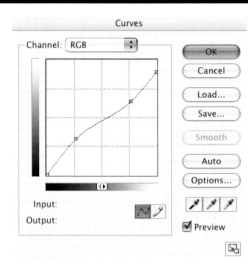

4 Late 19th-century photographs were generally low in contrast, so add a Curves adjustment layer. Click a point near its bottom end and drag it slightly upward, lightening the shadows, then click a point near the top and drag it down a little, pulling down the highlights. Some of Emerson's prints have even lower contrast, as though they were shot in twilight. To recreate this effect, drag the curve's top right "white" point downward and drag the bottom left "black" point upward.

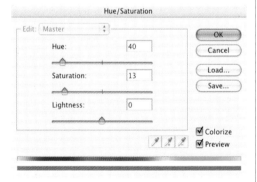

5 Platinum printing was rapidly gaining in popularity during this period, so add a Curves adjustment layer to simulate the typical platinum tone (see page 54). Alternatively, add a gentle sepia tone with a Hue/ Saturation adjustment layer.

6 If you want to add a little soft focus, activate the image layer and use Alt/Opt + Ctrl/Cmd + J to duplicate it. Name the new layer "Out of Focus" and set its blending mode to either Lighten or Darken.

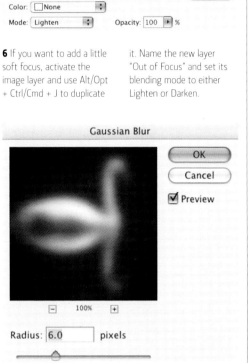

7 Add a little blur using **Filter > Blur > Gaussian Blur**.

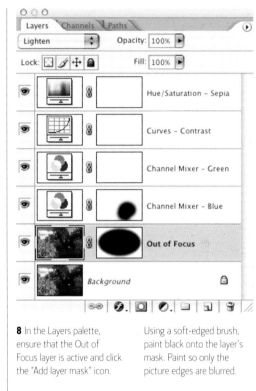

8 In the Layers palette, ensure that the Out of Focus layer is active and click the "Add layer mask" icon. Using a soft-edged brush, paint black onto the layer's mask. Paint so only the picture edges are blurred.

The Naturalists portrayed urban, coastal, and agricultural scenes in soft, understated tones.

Platinum paper

Platinum printing was invented in the 1870s. Like the cyanotype, the process relied on light-sensitive iron salts. These were combined with either platinum or palladium salts and coated onto printing paper, which was usually contact-printed under ultraviolet light from a negative. After developing, the platinotype or palladiotype print contained a metal image that was prized for its tonal quality and archival stability. For half a century, platinum was at the cutting edge of photographic printing, and was used by Emerson, Evans, Strand, Stieglitz, Weston, and many others. Platinum and palladium prices rose in the 1920s and made commercial production unviable, but since the 1970s there has been renewed interest in the process often considered to be the ultimate in fine art photography.

Platinum and palladium prints are distinguishable by their tone. Both are slightly warm, although platinum has a more metallic quality and, generally, palladium is more sepia in tone, with higher contrast. Imitating these tones in Photoshop employs the same technique as the cyanotype method on page 46—except that the curve's channel values are drawn from the table in step 5, below. So let's look in a little more detail at how you can take a toned photograph and work out for yourself the toning adjustments the curve should incorporate.

The first thing to do is assess a platinum or palladium print's tone. Perhaps you will be lucky enough to own an original, or be in a position to borrow one. If not, find a reference in a book or on the Web. Scan it into Photoshop or download it. Please note, however, that you don't need to copy or reproduce the image, just measure its color. Saving it to disc would constitute copyright violation, so please respect usage of the image.

I wanted to apply my platinum tone to this color photograph.

1 With the platinum print image open in Photoshop, select the Color Sampler from the Tools palette. Adopt the Point Sample mode from the Options bar so you can click individual pixels, mark their locations, and measure their colors.

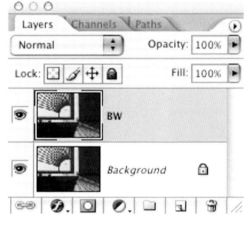

2 Hold down the Alt/Opt key and drag the original image layer to the "Create a new layer" icon. Name the new layer "BW" and click OK. Desaturate the BW layer using Ctrl/Cmd + U.

3 Zoom in so you can see individual pixels—to 1600%, for example—and use the Color Sampler to click pixels with three or four different tones. Avoid clicking pure blacks or whites—you need to identify a midtone, a shadow, and a highlight. Remember, the Color Sampler cursor becomes an arrow when you move over an existing marker, letting you drag and move it, or right/Ctrl-click and select Delete.

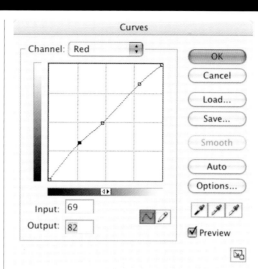

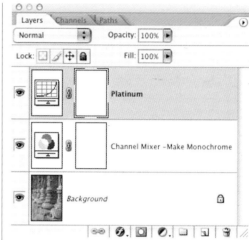

4 Examine Photoshop's Info palette—the lower section shows the RGB values for each marker. I reach for pen and paper at this point and write down the values for each pixel.

5 Next, hide the BW layer, and write down the RGB values for each pixel—these belong to the toned original, so have different values for each channel. You should now have a little table of "before" and "after" values. The next step is to put these values into a Curves adjustment layer, and then save it for reuse.

PLATINUM RGB VALUES

Marker	Channel	BW	Toned
1	Red	204	211
	Green	204	209
	Blue	204	197
2	Red	122	131
	Green	122	131
	Blue	122	116
3	Red	69	82
	Green	69	70
	Blue	69	57

6 To test these RGB values in a curve, reveal the BW layer, click the "Create new fill or new adjustment layer" icon, and select Curves. From the Channel drop-down box, select Red and click the curve near its top. Don't drag the curve. Enter the BW layer's first Red channel value, 204, in the Input box and the corresponding value from the Toned layer. Repeat this process for the other markers' Red values, clicking the curve and keying in the readings. Do the same for the Green and Blue channels, but don't click OK.

7 At this point it's a good idea to save your toning adjustment so you can use it again. Click on the Save button, then give your curve a suitable name and save it somewhere appropriate. When you're done, click OK to apply the curve to the present image.

8 Applying the toning to another image is very easy. If it is a color image, first make it black and white, then add a Curves adjustment layer and use the dialog box's Load button to call up the saved curve definition. The precise tone can always be fine-tuned—double-click the Curves adjustment layer and drag the curve's points, or reduce the layer's opacity percentage to moderate its effect.

Making a black-and-white picture look like a platinum print is simple—just add a Curves adjustment layer. The skill lies in making your curve recreate platinum tones accurately.

55

Gum bichromate

Popular during the 1850s, gum bichromate printing involved coating paper with gum arabic containing chemicals and colored pigment. When a negative was exposed onto this paper, parts of the coating would harden and, during development, the softer material would wash out. The photographer could brush and manipulate the wet print, and repeat the process using other pigments. It was only at the turn of the century that gum bichromate was revived, alongside other processes such as oil and bromoil printing, which enabled photographers to work in a more painterly style. Leading Pictorialists—Robert Demachy and Constant Puyo, for example—did not regard straight photographs as art, and retouched their photographs to emulate painting, manipulating the gum and adding pastels and other material. This approach was controversial—naturalist photographer Emerson attacked Demachy as "the great and original gum-splodger." The technique was soon to fall out of favor until enthusiasts rediscovered it in the 1970s.

To simulate a gum process print means imitating what Stieglitz described as its "unphotographic" method. The prints can lack photographic detail and are often a hybrid of painting and photography, like Impressionistic photographs. Sometimes brush strokes are visible. Demachy used pastels to add highlights, and many other artistic effects were applied. Image color varied widely from neutral to Clarence White's chalky reds, while Steichen's famous image of New York's Flatiron building has almost natural, pale colors. Art paper is particularly suitable for this style of picture.

Railway preservation societies are a great source of photographic subjects when you want to simulate old processes.

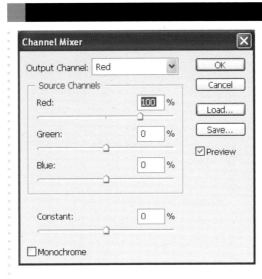

1 Make the picture black and white with a Channel Mixer adjustment layer. Tick Monochrome and adjust the sliders until you like the black-and-white rendition.

2 Add a new layer to the image and change its blending mode to Overlay or Soft Light. Now, by painting the layer with a soft brush, you can have the effect of dodging or burning, while preserving the original data. Paint black to darken the sky and grass verges, and use pale gray to brighten the train and other details.

3 Next, identify the features you want to retouch. Some gum process images were completely transformed, but more often they remained a combination of photograph and brushwork. Duplicate the original image layer by dragging the background layer onto the New Layer icon. Now, working on that layer, use the Marquee tool to make a rough selection around the train and sky. Temporarily enter Quick Mask mode by pressing Q, then click **Filter > Blur > Gaussian Blur** to soften the edges of the selection.

4 The Angled Strokes filter under **Filter > Brush Strokes** can provide a pleasing illusion of movement, while its Sharpness setting lets you produce more painterly results. Here I experimented with the Direction Balance until it matched the track's angle, and increased the impression of speed by changing the Stroke Length.

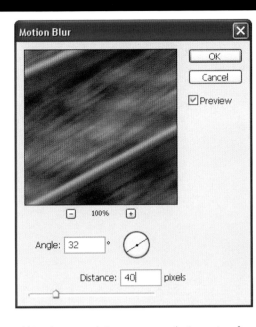

Motion Blur

OK

Cancel

☑ Preview

⊟ 100% ⊞

Angle: 32 °

Distance: 40 pixels

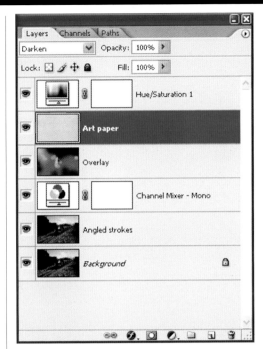

Layers | **Channels** | **Paths**

Darken ▾ Opacity: 100% ▸

Lock: ☐ ✎ ✛ 🔒 Fill: 100% ▸

Hue/Saturation 1

Art paper

Overlay

Channel Mixer - Mono

Angled strokes

Background

7 Finally, add a texture. One method is to scan a piece of art paper, and then drag the scanned image onto the main image. Experiment with the paper's blending mode—Darken worked best in this instance, as the lighter areas of the paper are hidden while the darker fibers remain visible.

5 Using the same technique as in step 3, select the other important retouching areas individually and vary the filters you apply. Try those in the Artistic or Brush Strokes group, or use **Filter > Blur > Motion Blur**. To convey the impression of movement, I deliberately blurred the track ahead of the train. It may not seem wholly realistic, but Demachy used a similar effect in a well-known picture of a speeding car.

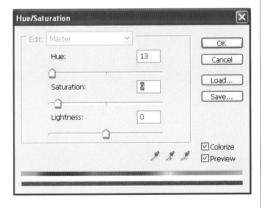

Hue/Saturation

Edit: Master ▾

Hue: 13

Saturation: 9

Lightness: 0

OK

Cancel

Load...

Save...

☑ Colorize
☑ Preview

6 Tone the picture by adding a Hue/Saturation adjustment layer and clicking Colorize. My tone was restrained, matching a Demachy print, but you could use much more vivid colors.

Gum bichromate prints could be extensively retouched while wet, and brushed to give an Impressionistic effect.

This picture's purple-red color matches some that I've seen, but artists of the time used many other pigment colors.

Autochrome color images

In 1907, the Lumière brothers introduced "autochrome," the first commercially successful color process. Glass was coated in a fine mosaic of red, green, and blue dyed potato starches which acted as a filter over a light-sensitive emulsion. During development, the emulsion layer became a black-and-white positive image, and the autochrome could then be projected or held up to the light, like an early version of a color slide or transparency. The process was enthusiastically received, and many photographers experimented with it, some of the best-known being Léon Gimpel in France and Frank Eugene and Alfred Stieglitz in the United States. Production of autochrome glass plates continued until the 1930s, when color film and printing first became available.

When you consider the characteristics of an autochrome, the most obvious is probably its Impressionistic or Pointillist appearance. Viewed close up, the colored particles can look rather like the color noise you sometimes find in digital photos. The particles also contribute to an overall softness, although this was sometimes the result of one-second exposure times and frosted-glass protective covers (you may want to simulate damage, too). In general, the colors are subdued and a little faded, in some cases unevenly.

Lumière manufactured autochrome plates for over 30 years and for many types of cameras, and no single subject matter predominated. Some French photographers used autochromes to record the events of World War I, but if you want a typical "turn of the century" subject, you won't go far wrong with portraits or flower arrangements.

1 In the Layers palette, click the "Create new fill or new adjustment layer" icon and select Channel Mixer. Tick the Monochrome checkbox and adjust the channel sliders until you're happy with the picture's black- and-white tones. Unlike other early processes, you don't need to bias the conversion in favor of the Blue channel—autochromists often countered daylight's blue tone by using a yellow lens filter.

2 If you feel the image contrast needs adjustment, click the "Create new fill or adjustment layer" icon in the Layers palette, select Curves, and drag the curve. This S-shape increases contrast.

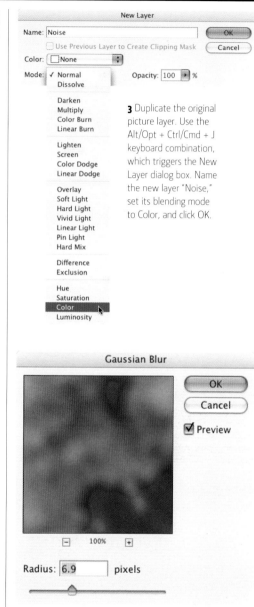

3 Duplicate the original picture layer. Use the Alt/Opt + Ctrl/Cmd + J keyboard combination, which triggers the New Layer dialog box. Name the new layer "Noise," set its blending mode to Color, and click OK.

4 Blur the Noise layer slightly by selecting **Filter > Blur > Gaussian Blur**. Use a relatively low radius of around 7 pixels.

58

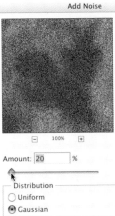

Add Noise

Amount: 20 %

Distribution
○ Uniform
● Gaussian

☐ Monochromatic

5 At this point it's very helpful to work at 100%. Use **View > Actual Pixels** or Alt/Opt + Ctrl/Cmd + 0 (zero), then move the picture so you can see a key feature such as the apples. Now select **Filter > Noise > Add Noise**. This represents the random mosaic of colored particles, so ensure Monochrome is not ticked and choose the Gaussian method, as this produces a more random effect. Set a low amount so that the graininess is apparent at 100% but less obvious when you zoom out.

Pointillize

OK
Cancel

100%

Mosaic

OK
Cancel
☑ Preview

3

Cell Size: 10 square

6 The Pointillize and Mosaic filters can be found via **Filter > Pixelate**. Again, set low values so the effect won't be overwhelming. If the Mosaic filter looks too uniform, blur it or add some Noise.

Autochromes were early color slides, often mounted and labeled, or sometimes framed without a back. They were comprised of a layer of colored particles over a black-and-white positive image—a clue to how you might simulate their appearance.

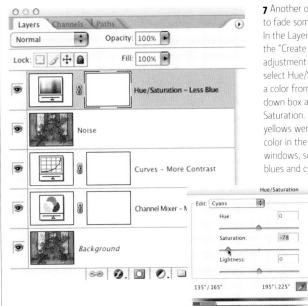

Layers Channels Paths

Normal   Opacity: 100%
Lock: ☐ ✎ ✛ 🔒   Fill: 100%

Hue/Saturation – Less Blue

Noise

Curves – More Contrast

Channel Mixer – M

Background

Hue/Saturation

Edit: Cyans

Hue: 0
Saturation: -78
Lightness: 0

OK
Cancel
Load...
Save...

☐ Colorize
☑ Preview

135°/165°   195°\225°

7 Another optional step is to fade some of the colors. In the Layers palette, click the "Create new fill or adjustment layer" icon and select Hue/Saturation. Pick a color from the Edit drop-down box and reduce its Saturation. The reds and yellows were the accent color in the apples and the windows, so I faded the blues and cyans instead.

8 Experiment with the Noise layer's blending mode. You could try Pin Light, but I found it too vivid fo r these flowers—as always, you need to trust your own judgment.

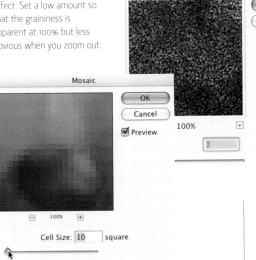

St Mary the Virgin, Dedham

American avant-garde

In the 1920s, many artists and photographers made radical moves to overthrow traditional or "realist" arts in a bid to be more experimental. American photographers such as Man Ray, and later, Edmund Teske, wanted to explore the possibilities of photography. Man Ray brought surrealism to the medium, with little regard for narrative or the conventions of reality. One of his most interesting techniques was solarization, which he began to explore in 1929. Solarization was a darkroom effect established in the 19th century—a process by which a print was exposed to light while in the developer. Some images look as though they are almost completely reversed, with strange, light tones in the shadows, while high-key images exhibit dark haloes around the subject.

Solarized prints vary depending on factors such as the image's tonality and the stage of development and period of time for which the print is exposed to light. The critical effect is the tonal reversal in darker areas, and there are a few ways to emulate this quickly. Man Ray's images often had haloes around the subject, a rather different effect. So you need to approach digital solarization in two steps—make a tonal reversal that suits the image, then work on the halo. It's worth remembering that Photoshop does have a Solarize filter, under Filter > Stylize, but it offers little control. It is applied directly to an image layer, so be sure you work on a copy of your black-and-white picture. You can try Edit > Fade Solarize and experiment with Fade's blending mode. Also try inverting the image after applying Solarize. It's still rather hit or miss, however, so here we'll use a more advanced method.

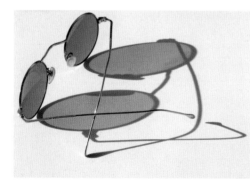

I captured this pair of sunglasses, on a piece of paper, in late afternoon light. I overexposed by one stop to create a high-key image.

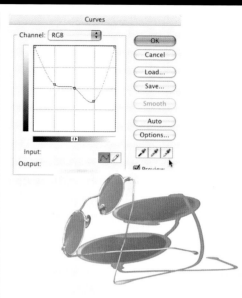

1 If your photograph is color, make it black and white by adding a Channel Mixer adjustment layer and checking the Monochrome checkbox. Using Red channel values disguised most of the texture of the paper beneath the sunglasses in this picture.

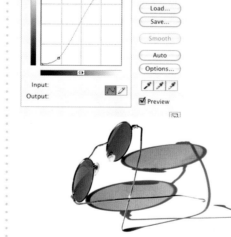

2 Consider whether you need to adjust the image contrast. If so, click the "Create new fill or new adjustment layer" icon in the Layers palette and select Curves. Many of the solarizations of the 1920s and 1930s isolated the subject, so I dragged the curve into an "S" that hid most of the remaining paper texture.

3 To add the tonal reversal, click the "Create new fill or new adjustment layer" icon in the Layers palette and select Curves. Click a point in the middle of the curve so a little marker appears and the midtones are fixed. Then drag the curve's bottom left corner up to the top left, so the curve forms a "U" shape. Adjust this to suit the image—I generally prefer more of a "W".

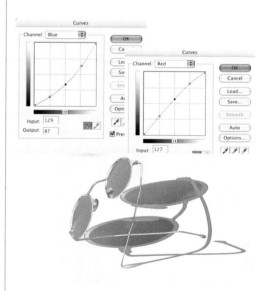

4 To mimic the gentle, warm tone of the gelatin silver print, click the "Create new fill or new adjustment layer" icon in the Layers palette and select Curves again. Drag the Red channel curve slightly upward and the Blue channel slightly downward, and click OK. Try the midpoints from the Red and Blue channels shown here as starting points.

60

New Layer

Name: Halo

☐ Use Previous Layer to Create Clipping Mask

Color: ☐ None

Mode: Multiply   Opacity: 100 %

OK   Cancel

5 Activate the image layer and use Ctrl/Cmd + Alt/Opt + J to copy it. This layer will be used to add the dark halo, so name it "Halo," and set its blending mode to Multiply.

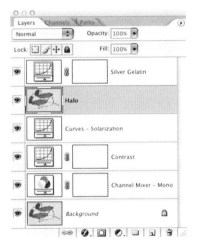

Layers Channels Paths

Normal   Opacity: 100%

Lock: ☐ ✏ ✚ 🔒   Fill: 100%

Silver Gelatin

Halo

Curves – Solarization

Contrast

Channel Mixer – Mono

Background

6 Drag the Halo layer up to just below the top layer in the layer stack. The toning layer from step 4 should be at the very top—it applies the tone to the Halo layer.

Threshold

Threshold Level: 182

OK   Cancel   ☑ Preview

7 Make the Halo layer into a heavy line drawing with **Image > Adjustments > Threshold**. Often this will result in stray black or white pixels, so a quick way to clean up the Halo layer is to apply a Gaussian Blur with a radius of 1, then apply a second Threshold adjustment to remove any shades of gray.

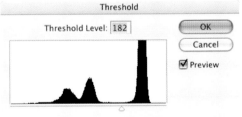

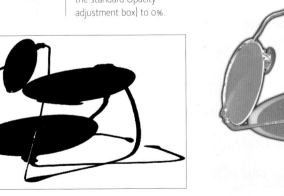

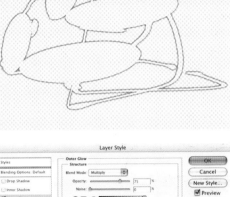

8 With the Halo layer active, select the Magic Wand tool (W), ensure its Contiguous option is unchecked, and click a white pixel. Hit the Delete key.

Layers Channels Paths

Multiply   Opacity: 100%

Lock: ☐ ✏ ✚ 🔒   Fill: 0%

Silver Gelatin

Halo

Curves – Solarization

Contrast

Channel Mixer – Mono

Background

9 In the Layers palette, reduce the Halo layer's Fill Opacity (the setting just beneath the standard Opacity adjustment box) to 0%.

Layer Style

Styles

Blending Options: Default
☐ Drop Shadow
☐ Inner Shadow
☑ Outer Glow
☐ Inner Glow
☐ Bevel and Emboss
   ☐ Contour
   ☐ Texture
☐ Satin
☐ Color Overlay
☐ Gradient Overlay
☐ Pattern Overlay
☐ Stroke

Outer Glow
Structure
Blend Mode: Multiply
Opacity: 75 %
Noise: 0 %

Elements
Technique: Softer
Spread: 10 %
Size: 24 px

Quality
Contour: ☑ Anti-aliased
Range: 48 %
Jitter: 0 %

OK   Cancel   New Style...   ☑ Preview

10 Click the "Add a layer style" icon at the bottom of the Layers palette and select Outer Glow. Set the blending mode to Multiply and the color to black, then experiment with the Spread, Size, and Range sliders to create a smooth glow around the object. Click OK when you are satisfied with the result.

Solarization is easy—just add a "U" or "W" shaped Curves adjustment layer to a black-and-white image—but high-key images also feature haloes around the subject.

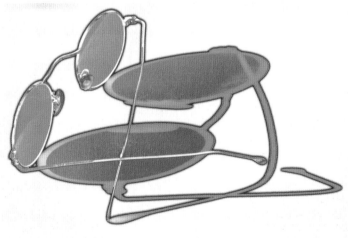

The Surrealists

Surrealist artists of the 1920s, such as Man Ray, often worked in more than one medium—but for many, photography was the ideal form for exploring their ideas. Torsos, hands, and other anatomical features were often rendered not as nudes, but as abstract forms. Sometimes they were stretched and distorted by mirrors or combined with other images in the darkroom. In one famous picture, Man Ray even painted "ƒ" shapes onto a female nude to make it look as though her back was a stringed instrument. With surrealism, the imagination was given free rein. Arguably, the classic image of the period is Man Ray's *Tears*. As its title suggests, the picture is a close-up of a woman's face with carefully positioned glass tears.

So, how do you emulate Man Ray's Surrealist tears in your own photograph? You can buy tubes of colored gel that simulates water droplets, but your subject may find using this substance an unappealing prospect. Instead, add artificial tears in Photoshop, and adjust them afterward to perfect your image. Incidentally, with a little adaptation this technique can be adapted to create glassy-looking text, buttons, and raindrop effects.

Many surrealist "portraits" were abstract close-ups, so choose a suitable readymade image or crop in tightly on your chosen image. This three-month-old was captured with a macro lens.

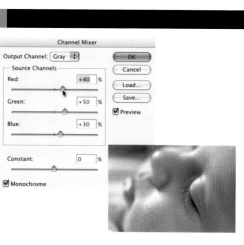

1 First, convert the image to black and white and fine-tune its contrast. In this case, a Channel Mixer adjustment layer produced a neutral, balanced starting point.

2 Once you're satisfied that the black-and-white image looks right, start adding the glass tears. Hold down the Alt/Opt key and click the "Create a new layer" icon in the Layers palette. Name the layer "Tears," and set its blending mode to Hard Light.

3 Select the Brush tool (B), reset it by right/Ctrl-clicking the tool's options, and adjust its size to match the size of the tear. Make the brush edges very hard by using Shift +] a few times, and set Photoshop's Foreground Color to white—hit the D key (which resets colors to defaults) followed by X (which swaps between the selected colors).

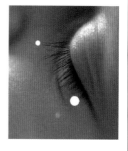

4 Zoom right in, check that the Tears layer is active, and then click the mouse to dab the face with the shapes of your tears. Adjust the brush size for different-sized tears, but realism isn't important; Surrealist tears can be improbably circular.

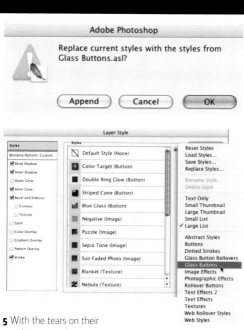

5 With the tears on their own layer, give them a glassy look with a Layer Style. Click the "Add a layer style" icon in the Layers palette, select Blending Options, and then click the Styles label at the Layer Style dialog box's top left corner. From its menu triangle, load the Glass Buttons style. Click OK or Append.

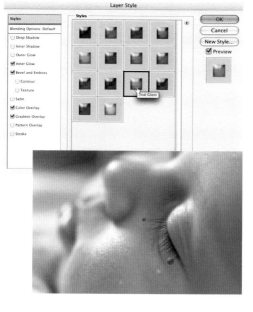

6 Set the Layer Styles dialog so that it shows thumbnails of the built-in effects. You can click the styles and immediately see their effect on your image.

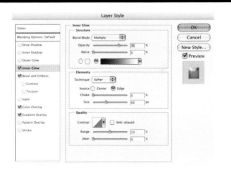

7 Here I've started with "Teal Glass," which has a colored effect. To counter this, first uncheck Color Overlay. This is not the only color effect in this Style, however.

8 The Inner Glow can also contain color. This preset style has a colored gradient, so click the little colored square in the Structure area to change it to black.

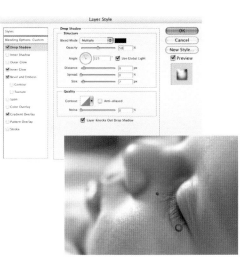

9 Add a drop shadow, but don't make it so pronounced that it looks as if the tears are floating above the face.

10 Just to give a faint edge, add a 1-pixel, mid-gray stroke to the layer.

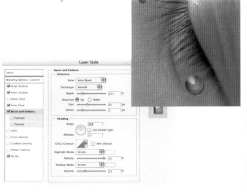

11 The Bevel option is probably the most important setting at this stage. Experiment with its Structure options until the edges of your tears rise into tight, drop-like configurations. In the Shading area, drag the edge of the Angle circle to simulate the direction of light on your droplet. Best of all, drag the crosshair inside the Angle circle and you can change the light's character, too—the closer it gets to the center, the more it behaves like a pin light.

The Surrealists often represented the body as an abstract form and added details such as these "glass tears." The sharpness of the tears contrasts with the shallow depth of field, and their artificial look and texture play up the surrealist effect of the image.

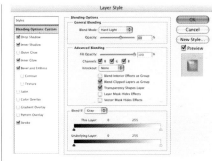

12 On Blending Options: Default, change the overall blending mode to Hard Light and adjust the opacity just enough to retain the fine hair on the baby's cheek—I used 60%.

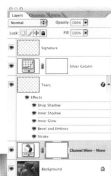

13 Save your style by clicking the New Style button (this makes it easy to apply the style to other images later). Now that you've styled the Tear layer, you can repaint your tears or drag them into position. The layer style updates the appearance of the tear automatically.

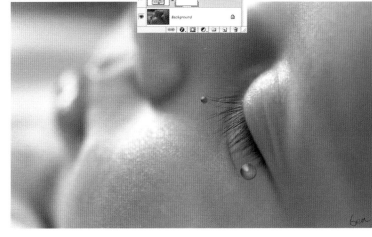

14 A great finishing touch is to add appropriate toning. Here I reused the gelatin silver tone effect we created on page 60 (American avant-garde). I also added a signature, using a small brush to write on a new layer.

Abstract cityscapes

The rapid growth of high-rise cities offered early 20th-century photographers fresh viewpoints and a new, graphic landscape. At the time, the emphasis was on technical purity combined with a more natural treatment, influenced by Modernist painting styles such as Cubism and Futurism. The greatest of cities was New York, which was most famously captured at this time by greats such as Alfred Stieglitz and Paul Strand, who photographed the city's people as tiny, hurried figures. André Kertész used criss-crossing streams of people to form abstract imagery. Realism and abstraction combined in this new style of urban photography.

To replicate this style, the first thing to do is look for high viewpoints: rooftops, upper floor windows, bridges, or any other position in which people are walking below. Photograph toward the light, overexpose a little, and turn people into silhouettes.

With this viewpoint it can be hard to make tall buildings look perfectly vertical, particularly if you're using a wide-angle lens. And even when you hold the camera upright, or just decide to use these "converging verticals" in your composition, you might still miss the one person who walks right through the scene. Sometimes you wait an age for someone to appear. So why not assemble the image on computer?

The shapes formed by the wall and the zig-zagging lights lead the eye up to the apartment blocks. Unfortunately, no one walked into the pools of light on either the lower or upper levels.

1 Duplicate the original image layer, then correct the convergence by selecting **Edit > Free Transform** or Ctrl/Cmd + T. Hold down Ctrl/Cmd + Shift so the image will be skewed, and click and drag the top corners to straighten up the building. If it looks a little squashed, click and drag the top middle handle. When you're done, double-click inside the image to apply the transformation.

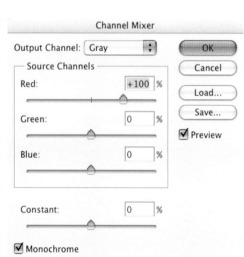

Channel Mixer

Output Channel: Gray

Source Channels

Red: +100 %
Green: 0 %
Blue: 0 %

Constant: 0 %

☑ Monochrome

OK
Cancel
Load...
Save...
☑ Preview

2 Next, make the picture black and white. In the Layers palette, click the "Create new fill or adjustment layer" icon and select Channel Mixer. Check Monochrome and adjust the color channel sliders until you like the tonal balance. In general, they should add up to 100%. In this image, the Red channel produced marginally more contrast, cutting through the morning haze.

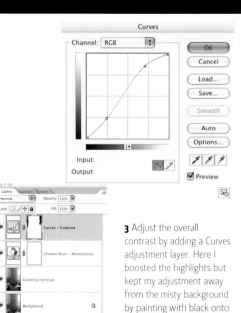

Curves

Channel: RGB

Input:
Output:

☑ Preview

OK
Cancel
Load...
Save...
Smooth
Auto
Options...

Layers / Channels / Paths
Normal   Opacity: 100%
Lock: Fill: 100%

Curves - Contrast
Channel Mixer - Monochrome
Corrected Verticals
Background

3 Adjust the overall contrast by adding a Curves adjustment layer. Here I boosted the highlights but kept my adjustment away from the misty background by painting with black onto the adjustment layer mask.

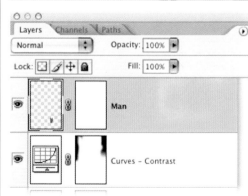

Layers / Channels / Paths
Normal   Opacity: 100%
Lock: Fill: 100%

Man
Curves - Contrast

4 Open an image containing silhouetted people, roughly select them with the Lasso tool, then use the Move tool (V) to drag them into your cityscape. Make sure the people are at the top of the layer stack, as they are in color and it will be easier to hide or remove irrelevant detail. Click the "Add layer mask" icon in the Layers palette. By default, this mask should be active—make sure the icon is shown in the Layers palette.

5 Open your new background image and hold down Shift as you drag the image thumbnail into your main picture.

There were better shots of this old truck, but its role here was simply to provide context.

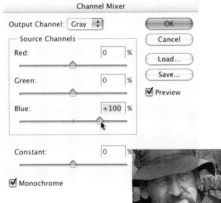

6 Move the new background layer below the main image and position and resize the two layers with **Edit > Free Transform** (or Ctrl/Cmd + T). To resize a layer without distorting it, hold down the Shift key as you drag the layer's corner handles. The man layer also needs to be rotated. Switch on the Grid with Ctrl/Cmd + ' and click and drag outside the layer's corner handles..

8 To remove distracting details such as the sheriff's badge, use the Patch tool. Set its options to Source, then draw a rough shape around the offending object. This will act like a selection—drag that selection to an unblemished area and release the mouse. Photoshop "repairs" the area automatically.

Patch: ● Source ○ Destination

Channel Mixer

Output Channel: Gray

Source Channels
Red: 0 %
Green: 0 %
Blue: +100 %

OK
Cancel
Load...
Save...
☑ Preview

Constant: 0 %

☑ Monochrome

7 Convert the image to black and white by adding a Channel Mixer adjustment layer. Remember, you can use this step to interpret the picture: use Blue channel values to make skin look tanned, or the Red channel to make skin appear lighter and softer.

9 To make the background look a little out of focus, duplicate the layer, then use **Filter > Blur > Lens Blur**.

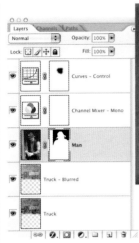

10 Fine-tune the image contrast with a Curves layer. Use the Burn tool to darken the man's hands and give them the desired weathered appearance. Last of all, crop tightly on the subject to create a portrait from your scene.

Depression-era photographers made records of thousands of ordinary Americans experiencing poverty and hunger.

Art Deco flowers

Flowers are an enduringly popular subject for photography. Some of the most memorable images were created in the 1920s and 1930s by two remarkable photographers, Tina Modotti and Imogen Cunningham. Influenced by Modernism and Art Deco, their flower photographs had a wonderful abstract quality.

Tight composition is typical of both photographers' flower images. Rather than showing displays of flowers in vases, they each cropped out the context in favor of focusing on individual flowers. Modotti is best known for pictures of closely gathered roses; Cunningham for immaculately lit botanical studies.

This bunch of roses was photographed every day for a week, sometimes in a bouquet, sometimes individually. No studio lights were used—they were placed in a corner that caught natural, early evening light.

1 With a subject as subtle as a flower, it's often valuable to examine the color channels before converting the image to black and white. The keyboard shortcuts Ctrl/Cmd + 1, Ctrl/Cmd + 2, and Ctrl/Cmd + 3 enable you to cycle through Red, Green, and Blue, then Ctrl/Cmd + ~ returns you to the RGB view. This rose was a lovely orange-pink, so the Blue channel was much too dark. A mix of red and green worked much better.

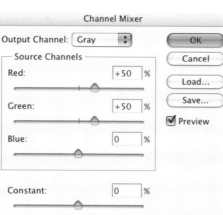

2 In the Layers palette, click the "Create new fill or adjustment layer" icon and select Channel Mixer. Pay attention to achieving a full tonal range, rather than looking at the final image contrast.

3 Fine-tune the contrast with another adjustment layer. Select Curves and drag the curve until the contrast looks right. Here, a gentle "S" curve boosted contrast a little, but also left the picture slightly soft and understated.

4 With closeups of flowers, it's likely that brightly lit petals near the edges of the picture will be distracting. Fix this on a separate layer. Hold down the Alt/Opt key and click the "Create a new layer" icon in the Layers palette. Set the blending mode to Overlay and check the "Fill with Overlay-neutral color" checkbox.

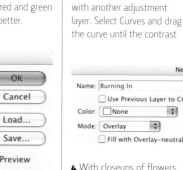

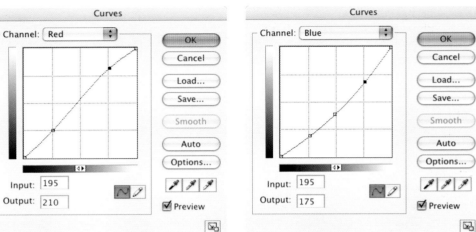

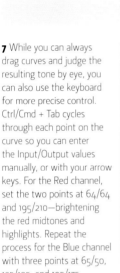

5 Activate the Brush tool (B) and make it soft-edged by pressing Shift + [a few times. Set the Foreground Color to black (D) and paint around the edges of the layer. You can adjust the overall effect by reducing the layer's opacity, duplicating it, or trying other blending modes, such as Soft Light and Pin Light. The difference is often subtle, as it should be.

7 While you can always drag curves and judge the resulting tone by eye, you can also use the keyboard for more precise control. Ctrl/Cmd + Tab cycles through each point on the curve so you can enter the Input/Output values manually, or with your arrow keys. For the Red channel, set the two points at 64/64 and 195/210—brightening the red midtones and highlights. Repeat the process for the Blue channel with three points at 65/50, 125/105, and 195/175.

Two pictures for the price of one: once you've shot your flowers, spray them with some water and you've got a fresh subject. If you forget, use the "glass tears" technique (see page 62) to add them in Photoshop.

6 To replicate the warmer tones of palladium printing, hold down the Alt/Opt key and add a Curves adjustment layer. Call it Toning or Palladium. In the Red channel, click the curve twice, adding two points.

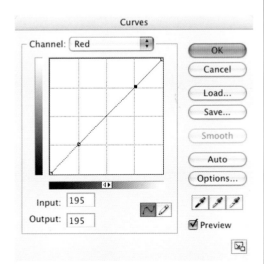

Palladium-based photographic paper was becoming much more expensive in the 1920s, but it was ideally suited to soft, gentle subjects such as flowers.

71

The black-and-white landscape

A classic black-and-white landscape shot seems so natural and realistic, it's easy to imagine all you need to do is find Ansel Adams's viewpoint in Yosemite, expose your picture, and convert it to grayscale. The reality is not quite so straightforward. Colored lens filters first control how the camera records the light on film, and the final print is the product of much darkroom manipulation. Adams was a master of such techniques, and imitating his style is a great way to appreciate the true art of black-and-white photography.

Adams's prints contain a full range of black-and-white tones, with visible detail in the deepest shadows and the most brilliant highlights. Clouds stand out against dark blue skies, and shades of foliage are distinguished in monochrome. Such tonal separation results from using colored lens filters to manipulate the light, and it's a fair guess that Adams would have applied similar techniques to today's digital color images. Instead of making lazy grayscale conversions, or simply shooting with a camera's black-and-white mode, he would have taken his time on the computer and used the images' color channels to produce these stunning effects.

Famous photographs tempt photography enthusiasts to visit locations such as Yosemite Falls in the hope of matching the quality of the original.

1 Add a Channel Mixer adjustment layer and check the Monochrome checkbox. The dialog box defaults to Red 100%—this means Photoshop will only use Red channel values to output the black-and-white picture. Click OK. Since blue sky contains little red light, the sky is now dark and the clouds much clearer. The effect is akin to using a red lens filter.

2 If you want to increase the effect, double-click the Channel Mixer adjustment layer and push the Red channel above 100%. You will probably have to reduce the Green and Blue channel values. Here, the sky benefits from exaggerating the Red channel.

3 While boosting the Red channel makes the sky look great, the green trees have become exceptionally dark and lifeless—they need their own black-and-white conversion. Temporarily hide the existing Channel Mixer adjustment layer and add another one, as you've done in steps 1 and 2, but using the Green channel. Examine the image carefully and identify the areas that are now improved. Here, the Green channel has lightened the foliage and brought out a fuller range of tones in the trees. It's like using a green lens filter on the camera.

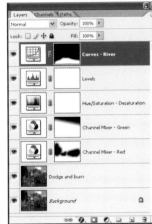

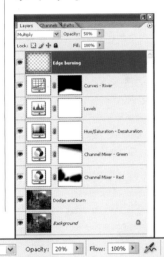

7 Darkroom printmakers often subtly darken the edges to balance or "hold in" the picture. Add a new layer and set its blending mode to Multiply, then paint with black around the edges. Reduce the Brush opacity to 20% before you begin painting. If the effect is still too strong, reduce the layer opacity to 50%.

4 Make both Channel Mixer adjustment layers visible. The lower, red-biased layer now makes the image black and white, and the green-biased layer has no effect. Activate the red layer's mask and use a brush to paint black over the trees so the red layer doesn't affect their color. On the green layer, use a Gradient Fill so that

it doesn't affect the sky. In case any color shows where the masks overlap, add a Hue/Saturation layer with Saturation at -100%. Again, examine the result carefully because you can infinitely fine-tune the Channel Mixer adjustment layers. Add to each channel or repaint the masks—whatever produces the most pleasing result.

6 Sometimes it's difficult to dodge some pixels while burning their neighbors. Here, the river's highlights still aren't strong enough, but further dodging would damage the weak shadow tones in the water. Instead, add a Curves adjustment layer and drag points on the curve until the contrast and brightness of the problem area look right. Ignore the curve's effect on the rest of the image—you can always paint black on the adjustment layer's mask.

73

Don't just throw away the color. Today, black-and-white landscape photography is about shooting in color and using the color channel values to produce the best tonal balance.

5 In his darkroom, Adams extensively dodged and burned prints, lightening some areas to reveal more detail and darkening others to create contrast. To enliven the reflections in the river, make a copy of the original image layer, select the Dodge tool, set its range to the Highlights option, and then drag over and brighten the water. Try the Burn tool on the cliffs.

Powerful portraits

Many distinguished historical and cultural figures are virtually defined by their portraits—just think of Yousuf Karsh's iconic image of Winston Churchill. Today, the trend in portraiture is for more spontaneous images, but the formal portrait has never really gone out of fashion.

Making a posed portrait look like it's been taken in a studio often involves manipulating the lighting. This may involve some fine-tuning—for example, darkening parts of the image and lightening others to make the subject look as though he or she is sitting in a carefully composed pool of light. Other effects are a little more radical and should always be done on separate layers.

This man, sitting in a café, was lit by artificial light from the right and reflected sunlight from the street.

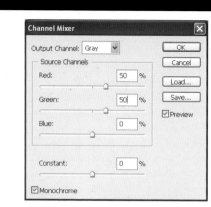

1 Make the image black and white but, as always, for the best results don't just convert the image to grayscale. In the Layers palette, click the "Create new fill or adjustment layer" icon and select Channel Mixer. Check Monochrome and adjust the sliders until you have the largest number of tones and the best tonal balance. Here, the default 100% Red channel value produced skin tones that were a little too pale, while trying the Blue channel produced tones that were too gritty. A mix of Red and Green produced a balanced result.

2 One quick way to improve this portrait, albeit at the expense of realism, is to flip the photograph horizontally. We are accustomed to "reading" an image from left to right, and, in the original, the man's scarf leads the eye up to the brighter side of his face and straight out of the image. Flipping the image makes you look straight into his face. Try it—it's a trick that isn't used nearly often enough. To do this, use **Image > Rotate Canvas > Flip Canvas Horizontal**.

3 Careful dodging and burning often improves a portrait, too, and the Dodge and Burn tools have the feel of classic darkroom tools. Duplicate the image layer, soften the tool's edge, and reduce the Exposure percentage. Move the tool gently, gradually building up the change. Set the Dodge tool so it lightens Highlights and brighten the man's eyes.

4 An alternative method for creating the dodging and burning effect is to add a Curves adjustment layer and paint onto the mask. Lift the curve and add more light throughout, then paint out all except the shadowed side of the face.

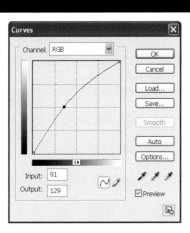

5 Curves also enables you to target certain tones, in the same way that the Dodge tool can have its range set to Highlights. This "S" shape darkens shadows and brightens the highlights. Paint the mask over the highlight on the man's nose.

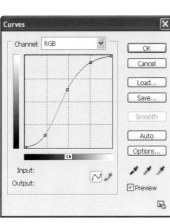

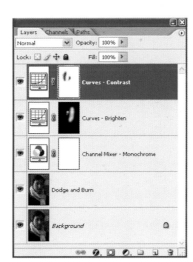

8 Starting from the subject's eyes, drag outward and release the mouse. The blending mode only takes effect once you've reached half its distance, and your finely tuned facial tones are unaffected. If you don't like the result, choose **Edit > Undo** and try again until the light is right. The Diamond Gradient produced the best result here. Reduce the layer opacity a little if necessary.

6 It's best to simulate strong directional light on a separate layer, as it will be easier to adjust or discard. Hold down the Alt/Opt key and click the "Create a new layer" icon in the Layers palette. Change the blending mode of the new layer to Overlay and check "Fill with Overlay neutral color."

7 Modify the Overlay layer with the Gradient tool (G) to create the new lighting effect. Reset Photoshop's colors (D). Choose a gradient—in this case, Radial. Set the gradient's blending mode to Darken, and make sure Reverse is checked so it starts with white and ends with black.

Flipping the image horizontally and doing lots of dodging and burning lends this subject gravitas. One trend in mid 20th-century portraiture was to crop into the top of the head—tighter crops draw particular attention to the eyes.

aximizing the mundane

While certain photographers may be strongly associated with one genre, many shoot personal images of other kinds, too. Usually thought of as a fashion photographer, Irving Penn created a stir with pictures of discarded cigarettes and decaying fruits and vegetables, and also undertook a series of ethnographic studies. More recently, Bob Carlos Clarke, best known for erotic portraiture, applied his eye to forks and mundane objects washed up on a tidal riverbank. Such photographers lend glamor and a surprisingly timeless quality to their sometimes unlikely subjects.

Pick your subject carefully—an ideal subject is one that is commonplace, often overlooked, with interesting form; I chose asparagus spears. A square-format print would be most appropriate, as would an expensive platinum printing process. Luckily, with Photoshop, we can emulate this style perfectly well without the same level of investment.

What could be better than an edible subject?

Not the most elaborate studio setup, but certainly an effective one.

For the new background, scan in some expensive writing paper, coated with oil, to simulate the platinum look.

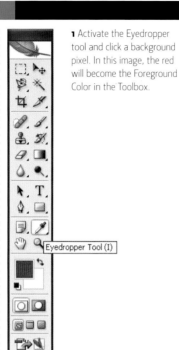

1 Activate the Eyedropper tool and click a background pixel. In this image, the red will become the Foreground Color in the Toolbox.

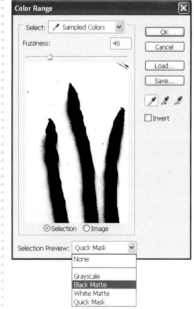

2 Choose **Select > Color Range**. The Color Range dialog box shows all pixels matching the foreground color. By holding down the Shift key, you can add other colors to the selected area. The Alt/Opt key has the opposite effect. I like to switch between the options in Selection Preview—sometimes Black Matte is most appropriate, at other times Quick Mask is best to show which areas are selected.

3 When the selection looks good, click OK. In the Layers palette, double-click the Background layer to make it a normal layer, and click the "Add layer mask" icon at the bottom of the layers palette.

4 The layer mask probably won't be perfect, and may contain scattered individual pixels. These will be easier to clean up if you view the layer mask on its own, so hold down the Alt/Opt key and click the mask in the Layers palette.

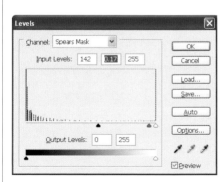

5 On the mask, paint with black to hide any remaining pixels. Boost the mask's contrast by applying **Image > Adjustments > Levels**. Push the black point slider a long way to the right, which will mean far fewer spots to paint out. When your mask is sufficiently accurate, click the image thumbnail in the Layers palette and move on. The layer mask can be fine-tuned later.

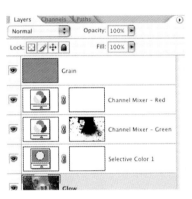

6 Open your background image, drag its thumbnail from the Layers palette, and drop it in the subject's window. Name the resulting layer "Paper" and move it to the bottom of the layer stack.

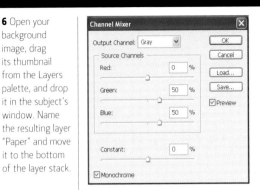

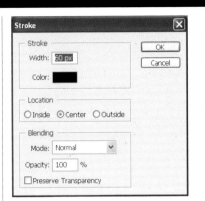

9 In the Layers palette, click the "Create new fill or adjustment layer" icon and select Channel Mixer. Check Monochrome and adjust the channel sliders until you achieve a strongly textured black-and-white look.

12 For a final touch, add a thick border. Add a new layer at the top of the stack, use **Select > All** and then click **Edit > Stroke**. This draws a line along the edge of your selection—set a suitable width and click OK.

10 To adjust image contrast, add a Curves adjustment layer. Lift the curve to increase overall brightness, then drag down a point near the curve's lower end. This produces a gentle S curve that increases contrast.

7 Zoom out a little to give yourself more room around the image, and activate the Crop tool. Hold down the Shift key and drag in one movement to make a square-format crop. At first, the mouse will stop at the edges of the image, but release it and then drag again, still holding the Shift key. Now you can compose the image—in this instance, increasing the canvas to the right of the spears.

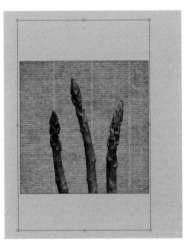

8 Resize and position the background using **Edit > Free Transform**.

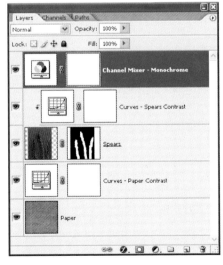

11 When your image is a composite, a single contrast adjustment may not be right for each original picture. So, for this image, add a Curves adjustment layer immediately above the Paper layer, so that only the paper's contrast is affected. Add a second Curves layer directly above the asparagus spears and hold the Alt/Opt key as you click the line separating them. This groups the layers and means that the new Curves layer only affects the asparagus.

Objects often look better in groups of three. Asparagus spears have subtle curves and can be photographed just as they are, or glistening with a spray of oil or water.

The age of jazz

Record covers, posters, and promotional stills amply demonstrate that photography has the power to evoke both an era and its sound. Asked to describe the typical jazz-age photograph, you'd probably think of black-and-white shots of performers in smoky halls, such as those taken by Herman Leonard and others such as William Gottlieb, Charles Peterson, and Francis Wolff—all of whom used the camera to document the music they loved.

You can't always get close to the stage at indoor performances—cameras (or just flash photography) may be banned, and you need such high ISO settings that your images are full of digital noise which becomes even more apparent when they are enlarged. There is smoke in the air, you are dazzled by stage lights, and, most of all, you've paid good money to enjoy the concert. Therefore it's often easier to capture great shots of friends or street entertainers and then jazz up the image with some digital magic.

Street festivals can be a great place for photography, but don't forget to enjoy the event.

1 Make the picture black and white by adding a Channel Mixer adjustment layer. Check the Monochrome box, and adjust the channel sliders (see page 72 for guidance on using these to best effect).

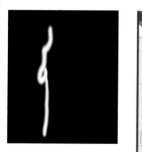

2 A quick way to darken a black-and-white image is to add a Curves adjustment layer and set its blending mode to Multiply. You don't even need to change the curve, but you can if you wish. Important image areas can be restored by adding a layer mask and painting the mask black with a very soft-edged brush.

3 Another method for darkening areas is to add an Overlay layer and paint areas black. Hold the Alt/Opt key and click the "Create a new layer" icon in the Layers palette. Set its blending mode to Overlay and check "Fill with Overlay-neutral color."

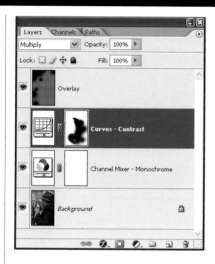

4 Use a large, soft brush to paint around the edges, and a smaller brush for more detailed work. Do as much dodging and burning as necessary to create an "enclosed" feeling.

5 Once the basic image is ready, add some smoke. Add a new layer at the top of the layer stack, name it "Smoke," and use **Edit > Fill** to make it completely black. Select the Brush tool and paint a line that roughly resembles gently rising cigarette smoke.

6 Select the Smudge tool and choose a soft-edged brush of approximately the same width as the smoke column.

7 Drag with the Smudge tool as though you were blowing and swirling the smoke. Keep changing the tool's size and softness—this helps to avoid obvious, repetitive shapes. You can also use filters such as Motion Blur and Liquify.

10 Go to **Filter** > **Noise** > **Add Noise**, check Monochromatic, and set the Amount to suit your image.

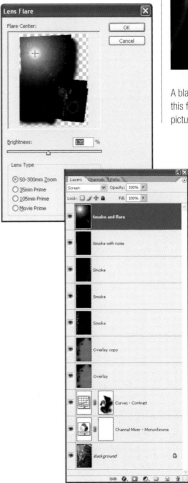

A black-and-white smoky atmosphere has been added to this former street scene. Consider adding a blue tone to the picture—or should one say a "blue note?"

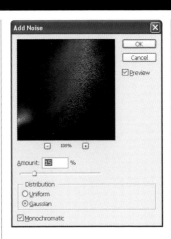

9 For extra atmosphere, simulate smoke particles in the air. In the Layers palette, hide all the layers that don't contain smoke, then activate one of the Smoke layers. Change the foreground color to white and the background color to black, and then choose **Select** > **Color Range**. Refine the selection with the Fuzziness slider and the dialog's eyedroppers, then click OK.

8 At any point, change the Smoke layer's blending mode to Lighten or Screen. If you like the result, the work's almost done. All you need to do is add another Smoke layer—make a new one, or simply duplicate your existing Smoke layer and smudge it again. Use **Edit** > **Free Transform** to stretch and rotate it, and try adjusting its opacity. Where two such layers overlap, you'll get nice swirls and highlights.

11 Another optional finishing touch is to mimic the lens flare from spotlights. Use **Filter** > **Render** > **Lens Flare**. This effect is generated in color, so use Ctrl/Cmd + U to desaturate the layer.

79

Photojournalism of the 1960s and 1970s

Photojournalism wasn't new in the 1960s and it didn't end in the 1970s, but, throughout these two decades, newspapers, magazines, and agencies such as Magnum offered a platform for many remarkable photographers to capture world events. 35mm cameras enabled photojournalists to get close to the action, and some—Larry Burrows in Vietnam, for example—paid for it with their lives. Don McCullin is renowned for covering wars in Vietnam and the Congo, but he also captured urban poverty and the plight of refugees in Biafra. Other notable photojournalists of the period include Ian Berry, with his Sharpeville massacre pictures; Benny Joseph and his work in the Deep South; and Bruce Davidson in East Harlem. These photographers went wherever there was news.

Emulating a photojournalistic style is a matter of finding your story, getting up close, and shooting a series of pictures. As Robert Capa said, "If it isn't good enough, you're not close enough." Violence or poverty need not be your subject—and, in this context, perhaps that isn't appropriate—but you can select an image from the world around you that you feel is best expressed in photojournalistic style.

Subjects such as these, taken at Speakers' Corner and a religious festival in London, or, for example, a happy occasion such as a wedding reception, offer you appropriate subjects for producing a good set of pictures. Individuals, groups, or crowds—shoot whatever captures the moment. Black-and-white photography is most commonly associated with the photojournalistic style, although this wasn't always the case. Generally, the pictures were shot from close up and with fast, 35mm, black-and-white film, which produced sharper, grainier prints. Once you've found your story, these characteristics are easy to apply.

1 Crowd scenes can present problems. Here the preacher was perfect in one frame—but two onlookers were looking down. As a genuine photojournalist, you would get fired for doing this, but nothing stops you from using faces from other frames. Open the other shots, roughly select each face and some surrounding pixels, and use the Move tool (V) to drag your selection into the main picture.

PHOTOGRAPHING PEOPLE

First, build up trust with your subjects. You win a lot of cooperation with a smile, a "Please," and a "Thank you." This Shiite parade, near Speakers' Corner in London's Hyde Park, was a tense affair. Nevertheless, some participants were happy to cooperate.

Be aware of the law. You don't need to belong to the press—in most countries, you can freely photograph people in public places—but you cross the line if you then use the picture to defame or exploit its subject. Always respect your subject's rights—pack common sense in your camera bag when you go out to shoot.

A wide-angle lens exaggerates the feeling of being right in the middle of an event.

When you use digital cameras for photojournalistic images, it can be a great advantage to show your picture to the subject. This helps to gain trust and enables you to stay closer to the action and get more shots.

Try to become invisible—not by being sneaky and making people suspicious, but by being confident and open. You'll soon find people return to what they were doing and forget about you and your camera. This image was captured by respectfully standing back, changing to a wide-angle lens, and snapping the shot.

2 Position the face with the Move tool and click the "Add layer mask" icon to the layer containing the face. Select the Brush tool

and paint black onto the mask with a soft-edged brush, blending in the pixels surrounding the face.

3 In the Layers palette, click the "Create new fill or adjustment layer" icon and select Channel Mixer. Check Monochrome and adjust the sliders until you achieve the right tonal balance. Here, a mixture of Red and Blue channel values darkened the lighter skin tones of the onlookers.

5 Paint on the Dodge and Burn layer with a soft brush. Your aim is to emphasize the central subject. Here, paint dark gray to burn, or darken, some areas. For example, to make the preacher's jabbing finger

stand out, darken the denim jacket above and below the finger. To draw the eye toward the preacher's face, choose a gray tone that is slightly lighter than mid-gray and lighten that part of the Dodge and Burn layer.

6 To give the picture a grainy, "fast-film" look, add another Overlay layer and apply **Filter** > **Artistic** > **Film Grain**.

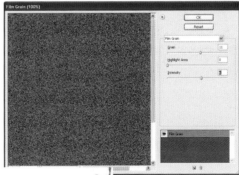

4 For maximum impact, crop the picture tightly and dodge and burn it. I prefer to do this on a separate layer. Hold down the Alt/Opt key and click the "Add a new layer" icon. Select the Overlay blending mode and check "Fill with Overlay-neutral color."

Almost any public gathering can present you with wonderful opportunities to practice photojournalistic techniques. Speakers' Corner at Hyde Park in London is an excellent location.

Surreal photomontage

Until the arrival of digital imaging in the late 1980s, photomontage was a laborious task. It often involved painting masking fluid onto photographic paper, exposing one image, then removing the fluid and repeating the process with other negatives. This was done in the darkroom and required precise registration of the images—and plenty of time. Artists such as Jerry Uelsmann, Philippe Halsman, and, more recently, Dan Burkholder, have produced amazing images in this way.

This pleasant image of a lake in Tuscany had even lighting and attractive reflections, so, in tribute to Uelsmann, I decided to add a couple of flying trees. I needed two photographs: one of a tree with leaves, and one of a tree in winter without leaves, to use for the roots. Most of the digital darkroom work is in isolating the trees from their surroundings, so it's a good idea to shoot some images specifically for such a project. Shoot trees against clear skies or very dark backgrounds—anything that will make it easier to cut them out.

This photograph, despite being taken in Tuscany, was rather plain and needed something extra to make it stand out.

For this project, choose trees with clearly defined backgrounds. The trees in this image came from Utah in summer and northern England in winter.

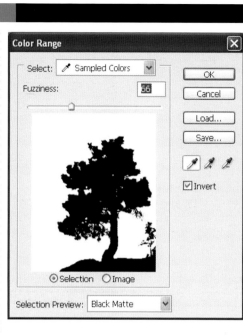

1 Open one of the tree pictures and use Color Picker to sample the tree's background. Choose **Select > Color Range** and then use the Shift key to click and add other, similar tones to the selection, and Alt/Opt to remove others. Adjust the Fuzziness slider until the tree is nicely outlined, select Invert, and click OK.

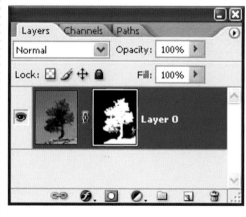

2 In the Layers palette, double-click the image layer, then click OK to dismiss the dialog box. This removes its locked background status, allowing the use of transparency. Click the "Add layer mask" icon and the background will be hidden, leaving only the tree showing.

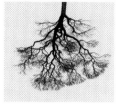

3 You may need to refine this mask. Click on it in the Layers palette, then paint with black to hide pixels and white to show them. For painting large areas, such as the rocks, hold down the Alt/Opt key and click the mask—only the mask will be visible. Paint onto it as before.

4 Repeat this process with the winter tree and then turn it upside down, using **Image > Rotate Canvas > Flip Canvas Vertical**.

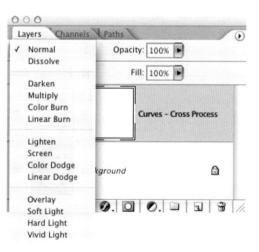

5 Open your main image and activate one of your tree windows. Drag its thumbnail from the Layers palette and drop it into the main picture. Do the same with the other tree.

6 Use **Edit** > **Free Transform** to resize and position each of your trees.

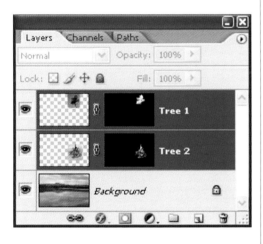

7 From Photoshop CS2 you can easily move more than one layer at a time. Hold down Shift and click each layer, then use the Move tool or **Edit** > **Transform**. Here, both trees are selected.

Adobe Photoshop

⚠ The underlying layer has a layer mask. If this is preserved then it will mask the merged result. Apply the mask before merging?

[Apply] [Preserve] [Cancel]

8 Once they are perfectly positioned, duplicate both trees and move one of each to the top of the layer stack. Select the top layer and choose Merge Down from the Layers palette menu. Click Apply and the tree and its "roots" will be merged into a single layer.

9 To make the reflection, use Ctrl/Cmd + J to duplicate the combined tree layer, then turn it upside down with **Edit** > **Transform** > **Flip Vertical**. Choose **Edit** > **Transform** to move it into position. If you also hold down the Shift, Ctrl/Cmd and Alt/Opt keys, Photoshop lets you drag the Transform box's corners outward, giving the impression of perspective.

Jerry Uelsmann's images are haunting—but don't ask me what they mean. Here, in my tribute to him, trees from two continents float over a lake. It takes a little care to extract the trees from their backgrounds, but then the possibilities are endless.

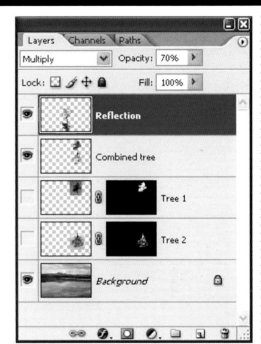

10 To make the reflection blend into the water, change the Reflection layer's blending mode to Multiply and reduce its opacity a little. If you need a shadow rather than a reflection, apply some Gaussian or Motion blur to this layer.

Tranquil landscapes

In the 1990s, there was a period of renewed interest in the minimalist style of Japanese design. Many fine art photographers were inspired by this spare Japanese approach, and began to create black-and-white images of exceptional simplicity. The pictures often depict islands or fishing poles and tranquil water, the result of shooting very long exposures at twilight or at night, lending images a meditative quality. Take a look at the work of Michael Kenna and Rolfe Horne—not surprisingly, Japan is a favorite location for these photographers.

While the final result may be subdued, high-key images are especially suitable as a starting point. Pick an image with an expanse of gently moving water and distinct, static details. Flowing rivers and still lake scenes can work fine; estuaries and peaceful shorelines, too; but it will be tough to smooth out rolling waves. Think of the Japanese aesthetic when looking for details—jetties, poles driven into the riverbed, isolated fishing boats. Twilight suits this style, but midday can work just as well when the weather is overcast.

This is a photograph of a floating gate, or Torri, on Miyajima Island in Japan. It was shot at midday in the middle of a humid summer—as you can see by the heat haze in the distance.

1 Start by using Ctrl/Cmd + J to duplicate the image layer.

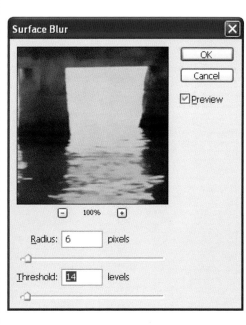

2 Apply a little blur. Photoshop CS2 introduced a new filter called Surface Blur that blurs smoothly toned areas, but respects edges. It's ideal for removing the details of flowing water while leaving still objects untouched. Choose **Filter > Blur > Surface Blur**.

3 Making this filter work is a matter of balancing the Radius and the Threshold of the blur. The lower the Threshold, the more the edges will be preserved. The settings here are much higher than you would use for smoothing skin details, but in this case the filter erases most of the water detail around the floating gate.

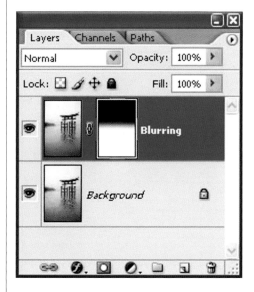

4 While a long exposure blurs the water, it doesn't necessarily blur static objects in the background. To exclude such areas from blurring, add a layer mask to the blurred layer and use the Gradient tool to create a black-to-white blend. Click and drag from the gate's base up, so that some blur still affects the background—after all, it is misty.

USING MOTION BLUR

During a long, twilight exposure, any clouds present in your composition would have moved. Select the sky area and use the Motion Blur filter to replicate this effect.

Motion Blur

OK
Cancel
☑ Preview

[−] 100% [+]

Angle: 45 °

Distance: 200 pixels

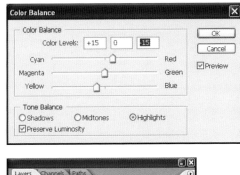

Color Balance

Color Balance

Color Levels: +15 | 0 | 15

Cyan ——————○—— Red
Magenta ————○———— Green
Yellow ————————○— Blue

OK
Cancel
☑ Preview

Tone Balance
○ Shadows   ○ Midtones   ⦿ Highlights
☑ Preserve Luminosity

7 Add a simple split tone by adding a Color Balance adjustment layer. If you want the off-white highlights to pick up a faint sepia tone, select Highlights and drag the Red slider to the right and the Yellow slider to the left.

Layers \ Channels \ Paths

Normal ▾   Opacity: 100% ▸

Lock: ☐ ✐ ✛ 🔒   Fill: 100% ▸

👁   Border

👁   Color Balance 1

👁   Curves 1

👁   Channel Mixer 1

👁   Blurring

👁   Background

Photoshop CS2's Surface Blur filter is probably most useful for smoothing skin, but you can use it on some landscapes to emulate a long-exposure stillness.

5 Once you've completed the time-exposure effects, convert the picture to black and white by adding a Channel Mixer adjustment layer. Check Monochrome and adjust the sliders. In this case, emphasizing the Blue channel produced a monochromatic image with less detail in the blue haze, and a higher contrast that emphasized the gate.

Channel Mixer

Output Channel: Gray ▾

Source Channels

Red: ————○———— 0 %

Green: ————○———— 0 %

Blue: ————————○ 100 %

Constant: ————○———— 0 %

☑ Monochrome

OK
Cancel
Load...
Save...
☑ Preview

Curves

Channel: RGB ▾

Input:
Output:

OK
Cancel
Load...
Save...
Smooth
Auto
Options...

☑ Preview

6 Adjust the contrast with a Curves adjustment layer. Use a gentle, contrast-increasing S curve, dragging a shadow tone down near the bottom left and pulling a highlight upward. In this image, the curve's top right end, the White Point, is slightly pulled down. You want the highlights to be almost, but not quite, white. You may not need to do this if your image is darker than the one in this example.

85

Fine art flowers

As still-life subjects, flowers are perfect. Photographers have many different reasons for selecting them: some photojournalists have turned to still life after one war experience too many; Imogen Cunningham shot flowers throughout her 80-year career; and, springing from Warhol's avant garde New York scene, Robert Mapplethorpe produced erotic flower portraits to complement his controversial nudes.

In black and white or color, many of the flower photographs of the 1970s and 1980s were lit softly from the front. Often the image was cropped down to just the stem and flower, and sometimes the stamen was suggestively prominent. The backgrounds were usually quite plain, although some featured angled light and shadows. They were typically in a square format.

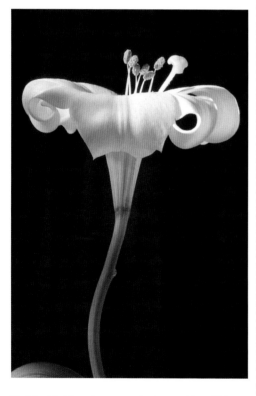

For this project the setup was very basic, comprising a kitchen table, mid-afternoon light, and a newspaper to reflect light back into the shadows. The curtains behind the flowers became a simple background that could be easily altered in Photoshop.

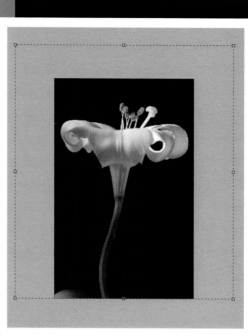

1 Give yourself plenty of room to work by fitting the image to the window with Ctrl/Cmd + 0, and then zooming out a little with Ctrl/Cmd + -. Double-click the image layer thumbnail in the Layers palette, activate the Crop tool (C), and drag it in a single mouse action so the entire image canvas is selected. Drag the right-center handle while holding down the Alt/Opt key, extending both the left and right sides of the canvas. Pull the top-center handle upward until you have a rough square, and double-click the image to apply the changes.

2 To make the canvas perfectly square, activate the Crop tool again and hold down the Shift key as you drag across the image. Using these two steps prevents you from having to go through the menus.

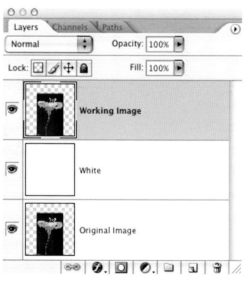

3 Duplicate the image layer using Ctrl/Cmd + J and add a new layer beneath it. This layer will later contain color, but for now fill it with white using **Edit > Fill**.

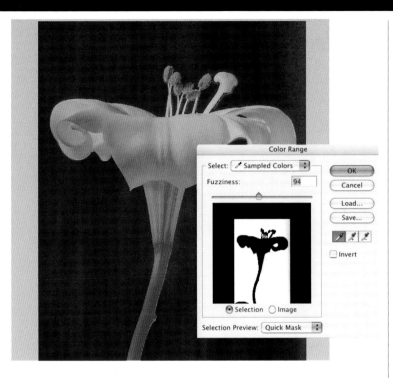

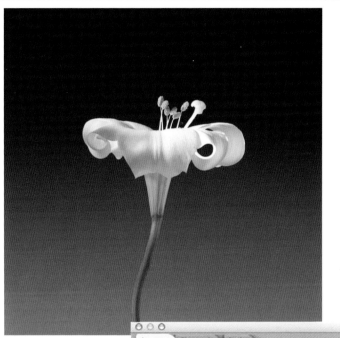

4 The more care you take to shoot the subject against a contrasting background, the easier it will be to select and eliminate the background. In this image the background is all a similar color, so use **Select** > **Color Range** and click a background color pixel. Use the Shift and Alt/Opt keys to add to or subtract from the selection. Setting Selection Preview to Quick Mask is useful—here, the red in the top right corner indicates that some pixels have been missed.

6 Once the flower is perfectly cut out, most of the work is done. Activate the White layer and select the Gradient tool. Set the foreground and background colors to two shades of the same color and drag so the top is darker than the bottom. Experiment as much as you like—these two reds look good, but cooler blues are even better.

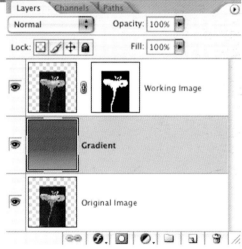

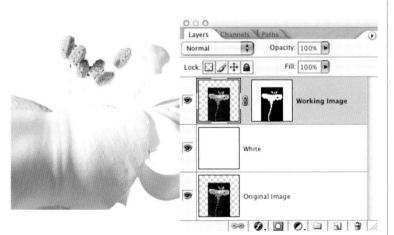

5 When the selection is as accurate as possible, use **Select** > **Feather** (Alt/Opt + Ctrl/Cmd + D) and soften its edge by 1 or 2 pixels. Invert the selection using Ctrl/Cmd + Shift + I, and click the "Add layer mask" icon in the Layers palette. There will always be pixels such as those around the stamen that need to be cleaned up by painting the layer mask with white or black—zoom right in and take your time.

Fine art flowers, continued

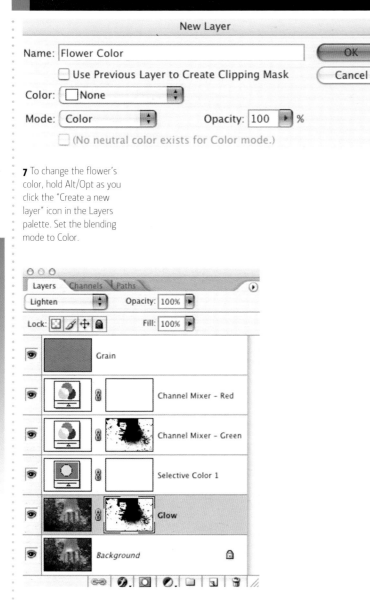

New Layer

Name: Flower Color   **OK**

☐ Use Previous Layer to Create Clipping Mask   **Cancel**

Color: ☐ None

Mode: Color   Opacity: 100 ▸ %

☐ (No neutral color exists for Color mode.)

7 To change the flower's color, hold Alt/Opt as you click the "Create a new layer" icon in the Layers palette. Set the blending mode to Color.

8 Make sure the Flower color layer is at the top of the layer stack. Without activating that layer, Ctrl/Cmd + click its layer mask. This loads it as a selection. Next, click the "Add layer mask" icon.

9 The Flower color layer mask makes painting a new color much more accurate. Paint around the petals with black to complete the mask (going over the stem and stamen, as we don't wish to color them).

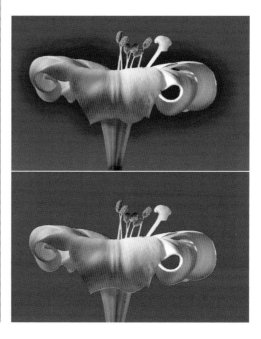

10 Click the thumbnail of the Flower color layer so the image (not the mask) is active, and paint with a color onto the layer—you don't need to be too precise as the mask prevents color going into the wrong place. Because the layer blending mode is Color, the underlying image shows through. You can also change the layer opacity.

FINISHING TOUCHES

Finishing touches might include applying Filter > Render > Lighting Effects to the Gradient layer. Make it look as if a spotlight is raking across the background at an angle.

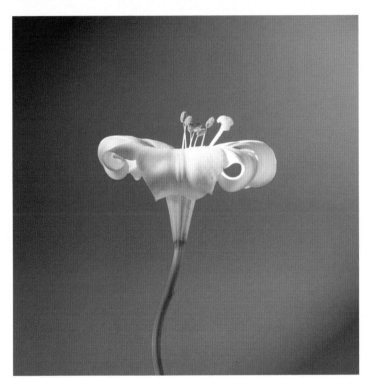

Lighting Effects

Style: 2 O'clock Spotlight

Save... | Delete | Cancel | OK

Light Type: Spotlight
☑ On
Intensity: Negative | 17 | Full
Focus: Narrow | 60 | Wide

Properties
Gloss: Matte | -67 | Shiny
Material: Plastic | -58 | Metallic
Exposure: Under | 0 | Over
Ambience: Negative | 20 | Positive

Texture Channel: None
☑ White is high
Height: Flat | 50 | Mountainous

☑ Preview

Layers Channels Paths

Normal | Opacity: 100%

Lock: ☐ ✎ ✛ 🔒 | Fill: 100%

Selective Color 1

Group 1

White

Background

11 As a finishing touch, add some geometric shapes using the Shape tool. Use colors that are already contained in the Gradient layer to create a subtle oriental feel.

Adding graphic shapes behind the flower gives this image a Japanese flavor.

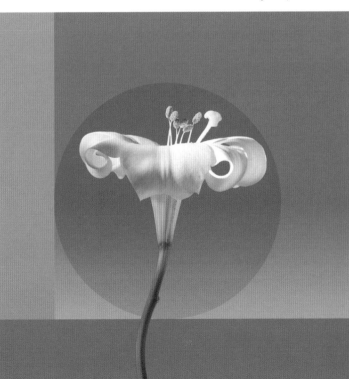

The kitsch and the quirky

While some photographers pursue classical beauty and others seek out the newsworthy, there are a few who make a virtue of kitsch and the exceptionally ordinary. Making tourists the focus of a composition shows what the experience of visiting great monuments—the Leaning Tower of Pisa, say—is really like, which today means recording the mundanity of the single remaining space in the parking lot. Through the eye of a skilled observer such as British photographer Martin Parr, such shots force the viewer to see something afresh. Grouped together and juxtaposed, they go beyond the quirky and offer a wider commentary. Parr has shot many images of tourists, food, and flags; Elliott Erwitt portrayed dogs and dog owners; Stephen Gill shot the unglamorous space behind advertising billboards—it's often a question of picking an everyday subject and persisting until it becomes thoroughly offbeat.

Cheap and nasty subjects typically have sickly sweet colors. Or perhaps it's the other way round and it's the color that cheapens? Imagine Las Vegas photographed in black and white—it might appear alternately seedy or high tech, but not necessarily kitsch. That's not to say that vivid color is obligatory—Erwitt shot mainly in black and white, and Gill's pictures all seem to be shot under overcast skies—but ultra-saturated colors really help to reinforce a kitsch quality.

After finding this souvenir stall on Westminster Bridge in London, it was just a matter of waiting until the tourists became oblivious to the camera, and for the sun to shine on the flags.

1 When shooting for this project, aim for an artless quality. Don't avoid bright, midday sunlight or try to rake the light across the subject—you'll be fine with the strong sun behind you, flattening the scene. Add flash if you wish, or emulate it by applying Photoshop's Shadow/Highlight adjustment. Start by making a copy of the image layer, because this adjustment changes the pixels and their color values. Use Alt/Opt + Ctrl/Cmd + J to copy the image and name the layer.

2 Select **Image > Adjustments > Shadow/Highlights** and adjust the Shadow and Highlight Amount sliders to lift the image. Aim to simulate the effects of a fill-in flash by increasing the Shadows Amount slider. (You may find that not all of these options are visible—click on the Show More Options check box to open the full array of sliders if you want to experiment.)

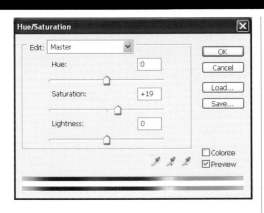

3 Although this picture was shot with a polarizing lens filter, the saturation of color wasn't maximized because the sun was coming from behind—notice the pale sky above Big Ben. The obvious way to boost saturation is to go to the Layers palette, click the "Create new fill or adjustment layer" icon, and select Hue/Saturation. Drag the Saturation slider a little way to the right, and click OK. If you go too far the result can quickly become brutal.

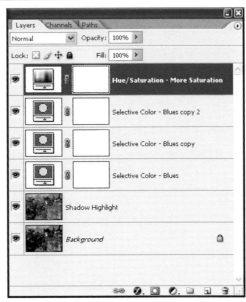

5 The Selective Color adjustment layer produces a much more natural color saturation, so try duplicating the layer using Ctrl/Cmd + J. The more copies of the layer, the stronger the effect—here I've made three copies. Complete the effect by moving the Hue/Saturation layer back to the top, as the stacking order makes a difference.

You can barely see London's Houses of Parliament and Big Ben behind this souvenir stall. Boosting its colors gives the image more punch, and also emphasizes its tackiness.

4 In order to make more subtle changes, try another type of adjustment layer—Selective Color. To emphasize all the blue tones, choose Cyans from the pull-down menu and drag the Black slider to the right, then do the same for the Blues.

The color landscape

As digital photography appeared on the horizon in the 1980s, film technology was also improving rapidly, changing the style of color landscape photography. Though no one ever wrote a song in its praise, some people refer to the "Velvia-like," highly saturated colors of Fuji's transparency film. As instantly recognizable as the cooler tones of earlier Kodachrome film, such color could also now be reproduced in print and on papers like Ilford's Cibachrome. The world had suddenly grown much more colorful.

The rich colors of 1990s landscape photography were not just due to film, of course, but to photographers' skill and their thoughtful use of lens filters. Warm-up filters change the white balance, which is easy to do to a digital image on a computer. But polarizing filters present another problem because they eliminate reflected light. This deepens the colors, something Photoshop can do in several different ways, but can also eliminate interesting reflections and make the picture lifeless. Cloning away such reflections is possible, but you might decide not to do so—sometimes you just need to swivel the lens filter so you get just the right amount of polarization that leaves key reflections intact.

I used a wide-angle lens for this picture. Its unusually shaped front element prevented me from using a polarizing filter.

HUE/SATURATION METHOD

1 A quick way to create punchier colors is to add a Hue/Saturation adjustment layer and drag the Saturation slider to the right. This works with some pictures, but can produce unnatural results. Here I marginally improved the sky's blue, but the rooftop became a garish red.

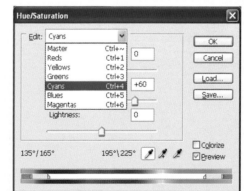

2 An alternative method is to adjust individual colors in the Hue/Saturation dialog box. For the sky, reset the Master Saturation to 0% and experiment with just the Blue and Cyan.

3 To remove oversaturated color from areas like this building, create a mask using Layer > Layer Mask > Reveal All. Select the Brush tool (shortcut B), soften its edges with Shift + [, and paint black onto the Hue/Saturation layer's mask.

4 For a stronger effect, duplicate the Hue/Saturation adjustment layer. This improves the sky, but causes unpleasant posterization elsewhere—a sure sign that for this project, Hue/Saturation really isn't the best approach.

Selective Color Options

Colors: Blues

Cyan: 0 %

Magenta: 0 %

Yellow: 0 %

Black: 100 %

Method: ◉ Relative ○ Absolute

OK
Cancel
Load...
Save...
☑ Preview

1 First, make the colors more vivid. Rather than using Hue/Saturation (see left), add a Selective Color adjustment layer, select the color you want to saturate, and push its Black slider up to 100%. I changed the Blue and Cyan.

Layers Channels Paths

Normal Opacity: 100%

Lock: ☑ ✎ ✛ 🔒 Fill: 100%

Selective Color 1 copy 6
Selective Color 1 copy 5
Selective Color 1 copy 4
Selective Color 1 copy 3
Selective Color 1 copy 2
Selective Color 1 copy
Selective Color 1
Background

2 Strengthen the effect by duplicating the Selective Color adjustment layer as many times as you wish. Here, I pressed Ctrl/Cmd + J a few times and made my skies a rich blue. Other tones remained unaffected.

Photo Filter

Use
◉ Filter: Warming Filter (85)
○ Color:

Density: 25 %

☑ Preserve Luminosity

OK
Cancel
☑ Preview

3 To simulate a warming filter, add a Photo Filter adjustment layer at the top of the layer stack. You don't normally want this to be too obvious, so stick to low-density values.

New Layer

Name: My graduated filter
☐ Use Previous Layer to Create Clipping Mask
Color: ☐ None
Mode: Overlay Opacity: 100 %
☑ Fill with Overlay-neutral color (50% gray)

OK
Cancel

4 For a digital graduated filter, hold down the Alt/Opt key and click the Layers palette's "Create a new layer" icon. Set the new layer's Mode to Overlay and tick "Fill with Overlay-neutral color."

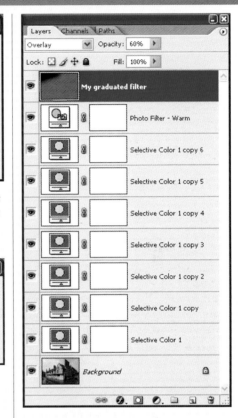

Layers Channels Paths

Overlay Opacity: 60%

Lock: ☑ ✎ ✛ 🔒 Fill: 100%

My graduated filter
Photo Filter – Warm
Selective Color 1 copy 6
Selective Color 1 copy 5
Selective Color 1 copy 4
Selective Color 1 copy 3
Selective Color 1 copy 2
Selective Color 1 copy
Selective Color 1
Background

5 The next step is to paint on the Overlay layer. Here I felt the picture was slightly unbalanced, and used the Gradient tool to add black to the top left of the layer. This creates a stronger effect in the darker corner, simulating using a grad filter at an angle.

The great thing about using Photoshop to apply a polarized, Velvia look is that you can choose not to clone out interesting reflections like those in the water, and you can saturate the color in areas like the sky. A polarizing lens would remove the reflections whether you liked it or not.

93

Lith printing

Lith prints are black-and-white with strikingly high contrast. In the darkroom, the photographic paper is overexposed and then developed in a thinly diluted lith developer. But it is snatched from the chemical before development is complete, leaving gritty shadows, few midtones, and usually gentle, warm-toned highlights. The technique was very fashionable in the 1990s, and is associated with top darkroom printers such as Gene Nocon, as opposed to photographers whose work is lith-printed. It remains popular in fine art and with darkroom enthusiasts, especially as a way of printing infrared photographs.

The precise tones generated by the lith printing process vary greatly with paper type and development technique. Most common is a sepia or pink tone, though enthusiasts often immerse prints in other toners such selenium, which can make them more red-brown. If your photograph shows a winter scene, change the tone (see steps 3 and 4) to a cold blue—in the darkroom this would require gold toner. Whatever tone you choose, high image contrast and the typical graininess of the shadows should help you achieve the correct appearance.

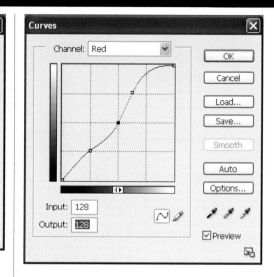

1 Make the image monochrome by adding a Channel Mixer adjustment layer. In this case, the Red channel produced the best balance of tones.

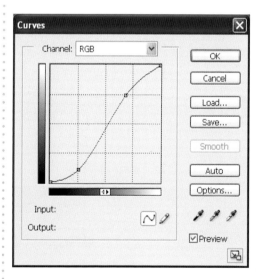

2 Lith prints typically have high contrast. In the Layers palette, click the "Create new fill or adjustment layer" icon and select Curves. Then drag the curve into a gentle S shape, darkening the shadows and brightening the highlights.

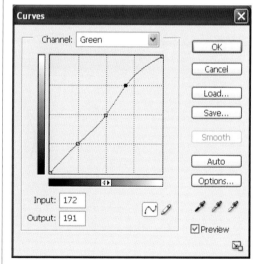

3 To add the toning, create a second Curves adjustment layer (I prefer to keep the toning distinct from the contrast adjustments). Select the Red channel and click a point toward the bottom of the curve and another near the middle. Don't drag either point, as their purpose is to leave the shadows unaffected by the tone. Instead, click a point toward the top of the curve and drag it upward a little, adding a red tone in the highlights.

4 Next, select the Green channel and add two points to fix the shadows, as in step 3, and drag the curve upward in the highlight area. As you do this, the tone changes from a red that you would not expect in a lith print and then goes through more appropriate tones until an unrealistic greenish tinge starts to appear. When you like the tone, click OK.

High-key images lend themselves well to the lith print effect.

94

5 The shadows in lith prints often have distinct grain; it is generally preferable to put the grain on a separate layer. Holding down the Alt/Opt key, click the "Create a new layer" icon in the Layers palette, set the blending mode to Overlay and check the "Fill with Overlay-neutral color" tick box.

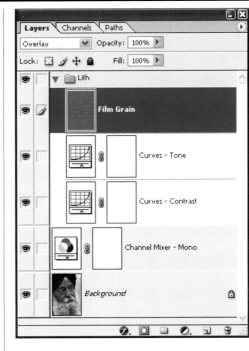

6 From the **Filters > Artistic** menu, choose Film Grain. The Grain slider has the most brutal effect on the outcome, and I prefer not to overdo it. Try the values shown (Grain: 9, Highlight Area: 2, Intensity: 6) as starting points—but the amount of grain is very much your personal aesthetic decision.

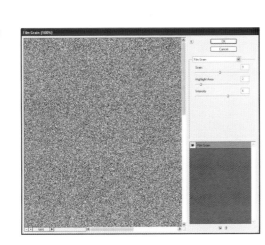

7 The Film Grain layer now has grain across all tones, but lith prints typically have smooth, milky highlights. Double-click the Film Grain layer's thumbnail in the Layers palette and adjust the Blend If slider. Drag the Underlying Layer white slider a little way to the left, which clears grain pixels from the image highlights. Hold down the Alt/Opt key and drag the left half of the white slider away towards the center—this smooths the transition between grainy and clear areas.

8 As usual, because all the work is done on layers, you can fine-tune the composite endlessly. One tip is to place the Curves and Film Grain layers into a layer set—you can hide them all or change their opacity with a single mouse-click or drag.

Smooth, sepia highlights and harsh, grainy shadows are typical of lith printing. With the method here you can fine-tune the image tone and keep the grain on a layer separate from the photograph.

Split-toning

hotographers have always toned fine black-and-white prints. The main reason is for archival stability, but more recently toning has been used largely for aesthetic reasons. Depending on the printmakers' choice of photographic paper and toning chemical, prints can be made warmer or cooler, gain purplish or blue tints, or reveal more subtle shadow detail. Split-toning is a variation that exploits how chemicals work on the highlights and shadows. If you interrupt the toning process, only the highlights will color, and the shadows can then be toned with other chemicals that work only on shadow areas.

For the digital photographer, toning can be used to convey a particular mood, depending on what the photographer wishes to express. The computer offers even more tonal combinations than the darkroom and enables you to experiment and undo your mistakes. What's more, Photoshop gives you the tools to explore different ways to achieve the same end result—in this exercise, you'll look at using Color Balance layers, Duotones, and Curves. Experimentation is good, and there are also classic effects, such as sepia toning, that are worth trying.

The London Eye is one of that city's most exciting photographic subjects. It can be contrasted against the Houses of Parliament (which sit opposite it on the River Thames), or, as here, simply against the sky and surrounding greenery.

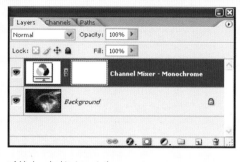

COLOR BALANCE METHOD

1 A black-and-white image is the best starting point for split toning. Use the Channel Mixer to emphasize the sky and clouds.

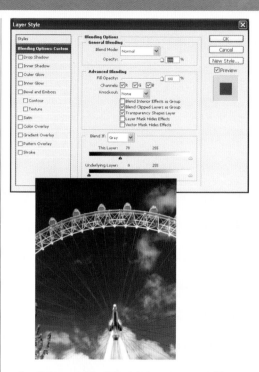

2 To put blue into the shadows, add a Color Balance adjustment layer and select Shadows. Drag the top slider toward Cyan and the bottom one toward Blue. Do the same for the Midtones.

3 Add a second Color Balance adjustment layer and select Highlights. Drag the top slider toward Red and the bottom one toward Yellow. The image color is now a blend, not yet split-toned. To create the split-tone effect, use one of the two following methods.

4 To split the tones, right-click the top Color Balance layer and choose Blending Options. In the dialog's Blend If section, drag the This Layer black triangle to the right. Don't click OK yet—notice how the shadows are now toned blue by the bottom Color Balance adjustment layer. But there is a nasty separation between the blue- and sepia-toned parts of the image.

96

5 To make this transition nice and smooth, hold down the Alt/Opt key and drag one half of the black triangle away from the other. The distance between these halves controls the blend and creates a true split-tone. This method is excellent because you can choose any colors you like with the Color Balance layers—not just sepia and blue—and the Blend If slider lets you control exactly how they meet.

6 Two Color Balance adjustment layers add one tone to the highlights and another to the shadows, and enable you to fine-tune your black-and white-conversion afterward.

DUOTONES METHOD

1 An alternative method is the duotone. While this is the traditional printer's approach, it destroys the channel-based adjustment layers. If you want to use this method, save your work in a separate file first. Make any changes you like to the image's shading, then convert it using Image > Mode > Grayscale.

2 Once grayscale, you can convert to duotone by clicking Image > Mode > Duotone and selecting "Duotone" in the Type drop-down box. Then click on the top ink and a Color Picker will appear. Choose a color.

3 Pick a second color using the same method. By default Photoshop will offer you the color picker for Ink 1 and color libraries for subsequent inks, but you can switch using the button on the right.

3 Finally, each ink has an adjustable curve. The tone of inks can be changed by clicking on the diagonal line between the ink's name and the color.

97

Infrared black and white

We can't see the infrared part of the light spectrum, but it can be recorded on special film or by digital sensors. Pioneered by the scientist Robert Wood, infrared film was commercially available from the 1930s. Minor White worked with it in the 1950s, but infrared really grew in popularity in the 1980s with specialists such as Simon Marsden and Anton Corbijn, whose album cover for U2's *The Unforgettable Fire* became a classic image of the period. While color infrared film is available, black and white has always been prized for producing near-black skies, clearly defined clouds, and shimmering, bright foliage. While some digital cameras can record near-infrared light, it is also possible to simulate infrared in the digital darkroom.

People always notice the unnatural tonal balance of infrared pictures—that is part of its great attraction. Trees, grass, and other plants are exceptionally bright because the chlorophyll reflects infrared light. Blues, such as those in the sky, are rendered as black, and haze is eliminated by the deep red lens filter that photographers used to cut out the visible spectrum. While grain is obvious, it is less so with some modern infrared films. The key to imitating infrared photography is to identify and convert foliage to black and white independent of other image areas.

Using Color Balance, as in step 2, is good with foliage and skies with good cloud formations. This picture also has many leaves—complicated shapes which would be difficult to select using the Lasso or Marquee tools, but well suited to this method.

Tip

To test whether your digital camera can capture infrared light directly, make a long exposure in a darkened room and fire an infrared remote control while the shutter is open. If it records an image, you can shoot infrared if you have an infrared filter for your camera.

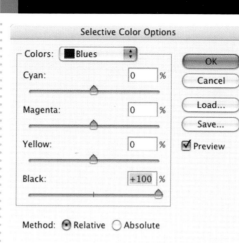

1 Prepare the color image by saturating the blues and greens, making them easier to sample. Add a Selective Color adjustment layer, select Blue from the Colors drop-down box, and then drag the Black slider to the right. Do the same for Cyan and Green, and click OK.

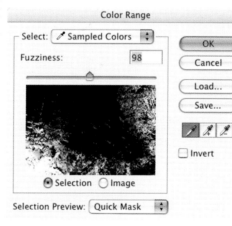

2 Selecting the foliage is the most important step. You can Ctrl/Cmd + click the Green channel in the Channels palette, or use the Lasso or Marquee to select trees and grass. Here the image has lots of small leaves, so it is better to use Color Range. Ensure the image layer is active, then use the Eyedropper tool (I) to sample a foliage green, and choose **Select > Color** Range. Refine the preview using the eyedroppers to add and subtract other foliage tones, adjust the Fuzziness slider until you have selected the foliage, and click OK. Sometimes the selection needs fine-tuning with the Lasso, but whenever you use the Lasso or other selection tools, make sure you feather the selection (this is not necessary if you only use Color Range).

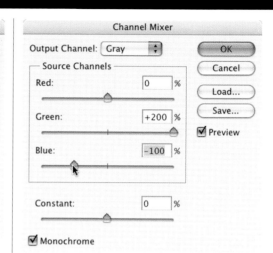

3 With the selection's "marching ants" visible, activate the Selective Color layer, Alt/Opt + Shift + click the "Create new fill or new adjustment layer" icon and select Channel Mixer. Name the layer "Channel Mixer—Green". Check the Monochrome checkbox, set Green to 200%, and one or both of the remaining sliders to the left so that the three percentages add up to 100% (allowing for the negatives). The foliage should now be very bright.

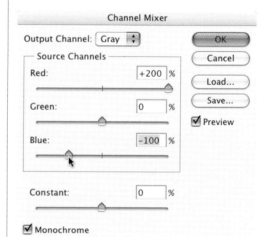

4 Duplicate the Channel Mixer adjustment layer with Red set to 200%, and Blue at -100%, a combination that makes blue skies black. If the combined values of the sliders add up to 100%, the adjustment will have no effect on the overall image brightness.

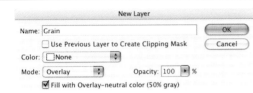

5 Film grain should be added on its own layer. Hold down the Alt/Opt key as you click the "Create a new layer" icon, name it Grain, set the blending mode to Overlay, and tick the "Fill with Overlay-neutral color" checkbox.

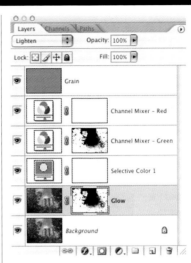

8 The glow radiates off foliage. This is already identified by the mask on the adjustment layer Channel Mixer—Green. So, without actually activating that adjustment layer, Ctrl/Cmd + Click its mask in the Layers palette so you see the "marching ants." Then click the "Add a layer mask icon" to add an identical layer mask to the Glow layer.

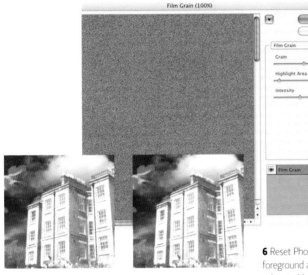

6 Reset Photoshop's foreground and background colors to black and white (D) and choose **Filter** > **Artistic** > **Film Grain**. Actual infrared film grain varies with film type and development, so there is no single correct setting. The settings shown are a good starting point, but if you don't like the result, undo it and experiment with other combinations.

7 For the foliage's infrared glow, duplicate the image layer with Alt/Opt + Ctrl/Cmd + J. Name the layer "Glow" and set the blending mode to Lighten.

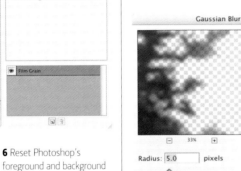

9 Click the Glow layer's thumbnail (be sure to click on the image thumbnail, not the mask), and select **Filter** > **Gaussian Blur**. Apply a small blur of 5-10 pixels.

Infrared black-and-white pictures are often described as ghostly or otherworldly. Some digital cameras can shoot infrared, but imitating the dark skies and radiant foliage is easy in Photoshop.

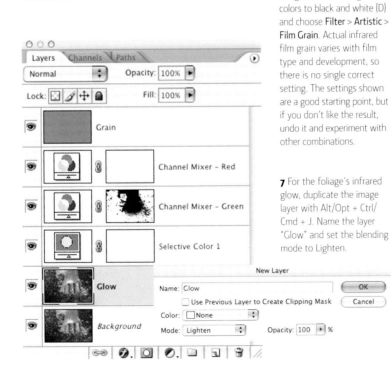

99

Polaroid image transfers

The Polaroid image transfer is another popular fine art photographic technique. After exposing the image onto instant film, the film is dragged into different shapes during development. The negative contains dye and is rolled onto paper or other interesting surfaces, creating an image that forms part of the material. Each image is a one-off, and can be manipulated and hand-colored. Many artists have experimented with the technique, including contemporary artists Jack Perno and Kathleen Carr, who has written a number of books on the subject.

A simulated Polaroid transfer consists of two distinct images. The first, a photographic image, is often distorted and rendered with the negative's rough edges. For the second, you need a textured image to use as a background surface. For this, it's a good idea to scan a few examples of fine art paper or cloth, or anything that might make a good backdrop.

The great thing about Polaroid image transfers is that you can make something out of almost anything, from portrait to still life—here, a vase with roses, captured in late afternoon light, makes an appropriate subject.

It's a good idea to buy sample packs of fine art inkjet paper and scan sheets with interesting textures, such as this one.

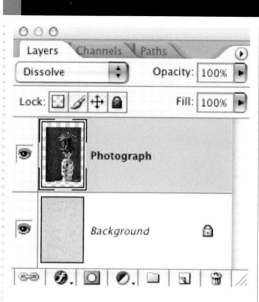

1 With both the photograph and the scanned background texture files open, drag the Photograph layer into the texture file's window. Be sure you can see the edges of the texture—if necessary, resize the picture with the Crop tool, holding down the Shift key to maintain the correct proportions.

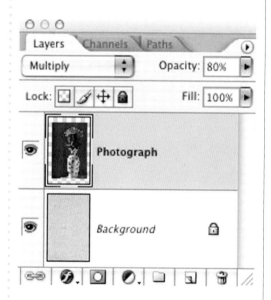

2 To make it appear as if the image were printed on the background texture, change the Picture layer's blending mode to Multiply, and reduce its opacity a little.

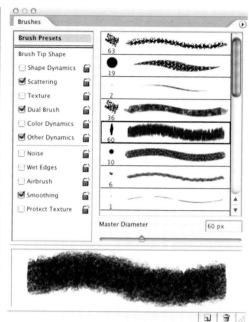

3 To recreate the rough frame around the image, I prefer to paint black directly onto the picture layer. Select the Brush tool (B), choose one of the preset brushes from the Dry Media Set, adjust its size to match the image, and give it a hard edge.

4 Reset Photoshop's foreground color to black (D). Click with the brush at one corner, just outside the picture's edge, and then hold down the Shift key and click the next corner. Photoshop will create a rough line between the two. Repeat the process for the other corners. For an even rougher look, you can hand-draw some lines. Make sure the original edges of the picture are obscured, and that the base is a little thicker than other edges.

5 Imperfections are often part of the transfer's charm. Experiment with the various options under **Filter** > **Distort**. Create a combined effect by applying one filter, then applying **Edit** > **Fade** immediately afterward, before applying another filter. Try **Filter** > **Distort** > **Wave**, set the amplitude to low values, and click the Randomize button until you have a gentle distortion that looks good.

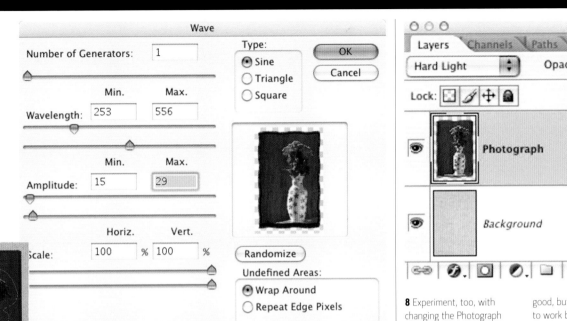

6 While a slightly stretched or distorted look is desirable for this effect, you might want to retain some of the image's subject. Check the Preview to judge the extent to which you want the vase

to appear to "melt." Use the Lasso tool to select the areas you want to distort, then apply the Wave filter to the selection once you've made a decision.

7 After applying the Wave filter, you can further enhance the results with the Liquify filter. Use the Smudge tool and set a low Brush Pressure in the Tool Options pane (to the right of the window). Now, stroke the brush over the canvas to apply distortions.

8 Experiment, too, with changing the Photograph layer's blending mode. In this case Vivid Light looks good, but Hard Light seems to work best. (Multiply is an alternative choice, too.)

Simulating Polaroid image transfers in Photoshop is quick and fun, and is almost as addictive as the real thing.

103

Polaroid emulsion lifts

Polaroid emulsion transfer is a fine art technique that produces delicate, uniquely beautiful photographs characterized by flowing patterns of fine wrinkles. It uses the same film as the image transfer method, but under hot water the image layer is peeled away. It can be placed on any surface, not just paper, and stretched and distorted before it cools and dries. Jack Perno and Kathleen Carr are two of the better known exponents of this magical process.

Emulsion lifts have apparent similarities with Polaroid image transfers. There is the same waviness and the underlying paper texture shows through the image. But these effects are much more pronounced, and the wrinkles are the distinguishing feature of the emulsion lift. Imagine the artist trying to maneuver soft, wet film as it dries and contracts onto the paper—it's a mixture of skill and accident. Some wrinkles are fine ripples, while others are more like folds where the image color is multiplied. This is the key feature, but don't overlook the clear border around the image and the physical edge of the film which you can see on the surface of the paper.

Choose a picture with lots of lighter-toned areas—the distinctive, flowing wrinkles are less obvious in the shadows.

1 First, a few preparatory steps. Add the clear film border by choosing **Image** > **Canvas Size**. Check Relative and set the Canvas Extension Color to white.

2 Open the paper texture file and drag its image layer onto your photograph. Name the layer "Art Paper" and resize it so it fills the canvas—use **Edit** > **Free Transform** or Ctrl/Cmd + T.

3 Copy the photograph layer using Alt/Opt + Ctrl/Cmd + J, name the layer "Lift," and changing its blending mode to Multiply. In the Layers palette, move the Lift layer to the top of the layer stack.

4 Press Q and activate the Quick Mask. Select the whole canvas with Ctrl/Cmd + A and hit the Delete key, so the Quick Mask fills the image with its red overlay.

5 In the Brushes palette, load the Square Brushes set and pick a small, hard-edged brush such as "Hard Square 10 pixels." Set its Opacity and Fill options to 100%.

6 Now the creative part begins! Be sure that the foreground color is white, and draw lots of lines on the mask. Imagine drawing fine wrinkles in soft film. In general, avoid the main subject. Also draw into the clear white border. Notice here how one of my lines roughly echoed the lamp.

7 To simulate a few of the larger, overlapping or folded wrinkles, choose the standard Lasso tool and drag so you create a thin, elongated selection. I made this selection in a single drag operation, criss-crossing randomly.

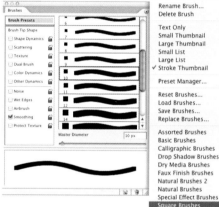

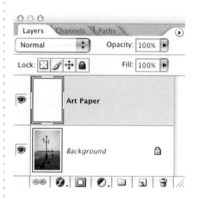

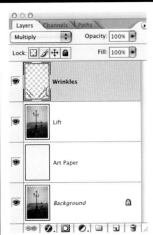

8 Switch to the Fill tool and click once inside the selection to fill it with white. Next, make another section and repeat this process a few times, so that the mask reveals a mixture of the fine and folded wrinkles.

9 When you're done, hit the Q key again to switch off the Quick Mask. Use Alt/ Opt + Ctrl/Cmd + J to copy the selection into a new Wrinkles layer. Set the blending mode to Multiply.

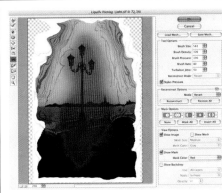

12 From this point onward, the steps are similar to the image transfer technique on page 104–5, only a little more radical. Use the Lasso tool to select those areas that you want to distort— here I selected the street lamp and then used **Select > Inverse** to select the rest of the picture. Next, apply **Filter > Distort > Wave**, setting the amplitude and other settings to low values, and clicking the Randomize button until it looks like soft, wet film.

13 Now select **Filter > Liquify** and be rough— soft, wet film is not easy to handle. I prefer the Turbulence tool with a large brush size. Drag so that the wrinkles are twisted, and squeeze them against one another. To create a more

realistic physical film edge, I also like to gently drag in all the edges, even where I've not done much other distortion. Notice, too, how the unselected central area has a red overlay and is protected. When you're done, click OK.

Levels

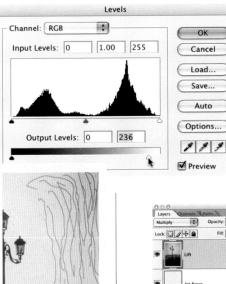

10 Be sure that the Wrinkles layer is active, then choose **Image > Adjustments > Levels** and drag the Output Levels white triangle to the left—just enough to make the wrinkles visible in the clear white border.

14 Finally, double-click the Lift layer's thumbnail and adjust the layer style. Add a thin, dark gray stroke that simulates the film's physical edge. You should also reduce the opacity to 80–90%.

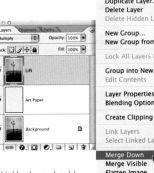

Tip

Save your Wrinkles selection as an alpha channel for reuse. It could even become a starting point for adding a similar effect to another image.

11 The Wrinkles layer should still be active, so merge it into the Lift layer using Ctrl/Cmd + E.

Simulating emulsion lifts in Photoshop isn't difficult but is largely a manual process, reflecting the way an artist positions and distorts the soft Polaroid emulsion layer onto art paper.

The joiner

In the pre-digital era, it was fun to see your pictures immediately with the aid of Polaroid instant film, and it is still used in professional photography for test exposures to cut down film costs. Artists have exploited the material, scratching, scraping, and separating its layers. The joiner is another clever technique, taking multiple shots of a scene and assembling them into a collage. Made famous by David Hockney, in his hands the joiner had echoes of Cubism and reverse perspective, where objects are larger when they are closer to the point of view.

A joiner is different from a "stitched" photograph. It is recognizably composed of its individual pictures, which form a collage of squares, overlapping like fish scales and casting small drop shadows. Depending on the camera and lens quality, the pictures may be vignetted or darkened around the edges, giving the composite a beveled character. Your choice of subject is endless, but the effect probably works best when the composition has a wide-angle view, with features scattered around the frame.

You can assemble your joiner from a series of shots. This requires a camera that can shoot lots of photos in a burst, which requires more computer memory and yields a larger final image. Alternatively, you can break a single photograph up into squares and maneuver them as if they were separate prints. This is the approach I'll follow here, because it's easy to adapt it to collages of multiple originals. You may want to combine the two approaches and build your joiner from squares drawn from two or more originals. There are no rules.

106

A balloon festival is a great photographic subject, but look for any image with a wide angle of view.

1 Starting with the original image, create a new layer and fill it with white, then copy your original picture layer and move it to the top of the layer stack. Name the copied layer "Source."

2 From the Layers palette, click the "Add a layer style" icon, and add a drop shadow and a thin, gray stroke. Click OK. You won't be able to see any visible difference, but it makes the next steps easier.

3 Select the Marquee tool (M) and set its width and height to "500px" in the Tool Options bar. The "px" stands for pixel—you should adjust the value depending on what size "photos" you want.

4 Select one part of the image and use Ctrl/Cmd + J to copy the selection into its own layer. You'll see that the new layer automatically has the same layer style as the Source.

5 Activate the Source layer, and repeat step 4 as many times as you wish. At any point, you can review progress by switching off the Source layer's visibility. Your squares should overlap a bit.

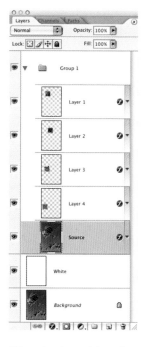

6 You will end up with lots of layers containing square sections cut from the main image. As the Layers palette can become quite unwieldy, gather layers into sets, which you can collapse or expand with a single click on the group's arrow. If you put the Source layer inside the group, all new layers created from the Source will also be added there.

7 Keep toggling the Source layer's visibility and adding layers until the basic composition looks right. Deliberately leave gaps. When you're done, hide the Source layer..

8 Activate each layer, then select **Edit > Free Transform** or Ctrl/Cmd + T, and adjust the layer's position. You can rotate the images by dragging just outside the corners. Leave some layers alone, too.

9 There is a fair chance that you will want to fine-tune the drop shadow effect you added to each square in step 2. Or you may want to darken the edges of the square. Activate the first layer and add an Inner Glow layer style.

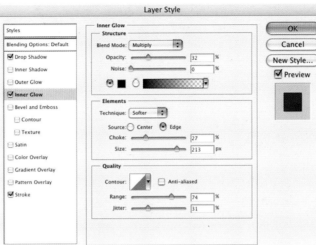

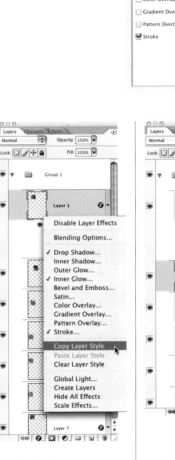

10 Instead of repeating step 9 for each layer, right/Ctrl-click your updated layer and select **Copy Layer Style**.

11 You may then right/Ctrl-click each layer and select **Paste Layer Style**. However, that's inefficient, and you may want to update the style again. In Photoshop CS2, you can select multiple layers using Shift-click or Ctrl/Cmd + click. In earlier versions you'll need to link the layers, then right/Ctrl-click and paste the style to all at once.

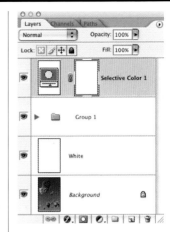

12 Once the layer styles are defined, you can fine-tune the position of the squares as much as you like.

In a joiner, the eye jumps from one interesting detail to another, so the viewer's experience is more "staccato" than with a single image.

Cross-processing

Cross-processing is developing color print or slide film in the wrong chemicals—for example, color negative film in slide chemicals ("C-41 as E-6") or slide film by the color negative process ("E-6 as C-41"). Not surprisingly, this causes wild color and contrast shifts and requires lots of trial and error. But for a period in the 1980s and 1990s, cross-processed images were very much the vogue, with Nick Knight's fashion and studio work being arguably the most influential.

With many possible permutations of film stock and processing technique, there is no single, identifiable, cross-processed appearance. The most common combination is C-41 as E-6, in which slide chemistry is used to process color negative film, and it's a quick job to imitate it in Photoshop. Image contrast is usually high with blown-out highlights, while the shadows tend toward dense shades of blue. Reds tend to be magenta, lips almost purple, and highlights normally have a yellow-green color cast. As for subject matter, try fashion or portraiture, but there's no need to restrict your imagination.

I chose an elegant outdoor portrait shot—the skin tones and red lipstick look especially striking in cross-processed images.

Tip

To save your curve to a file on your hard drive, just click the Save button. Applying the same cross-processing adjustment to other images is a simple matter of loading it with the Load button in the Curves dialog box.

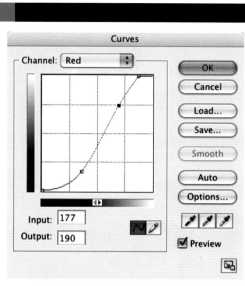

1 With the original image open, click the "Create new fill or new adjustment layer" icon in the Layers palette and select Curves. From the Channel drop-down box, select the Red channel and drag the top right of the curve a little to the left. Then drag a couple of points on the curve so that it forms a very gentle S—darkening the shadows and brightening the Red channel's highlights.

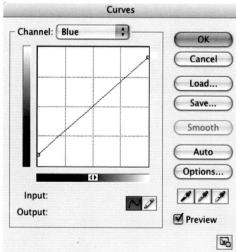

2 Select the Blue channel and drag the curve's top-right point downward. It doesn't need to be much—just enough to take some blue out of the highlights. Then drag the curve's bottom-right point up a little, blocking up the Blue channel in the shadows.

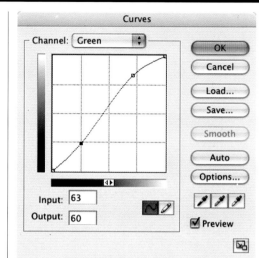

3 In the Green channel, add another gentle S curve—increasing the contrast, especially in the highlights.

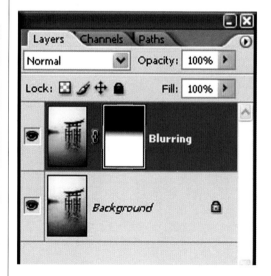

4 Fine-tune the channel curves to suit your image, but leave the combined RGB curve untouched. Focus on the color balance rather than the contrast, which you can fix later, in step 6.

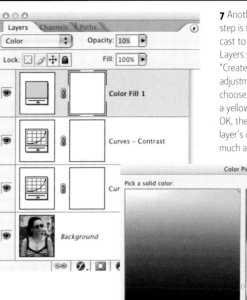

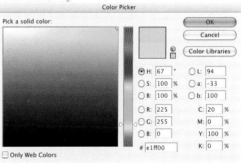

7 Another optional final step is to add a yellow color cast to the picture. In the Layers palette, click the "Create new fill or new adjustment layer" icon and choose Solid Color. Select a yellow-green and click OK, then reduce the new layer's opacity—10% is as much as you'll need.

5 Blown highlights are a common—if not always welcome—characteristic of C-41 as E-6 cross-processing. They should result from the contrast-increasing curves used in steps 1–3, but in Photoshop it's possible to eliminate them if you wish. Try changing the Curves adjustment layer's blending mode to Color and the image will combine the color shifts with the image's original luminosity.

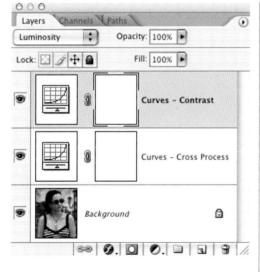

6 If you need to fine-tune the image contrast, add a Curves adjustment layer and set its blending mode to Luminosity so it doesn't cause any further color shifts.

This image was digitally captured and had daylight white balance. In Photoshop you can simulate 1980s-style cross-processing and add the film rebate (border)—another typical affectation of the era.

PAINTERS & PRINTMAKERS

How to create images
in the style of the
world's greatest artists

Intaglio

PAINTERS & PRINTMAKERS

Printing as we know it has developed from Johannes Gutenberg's 15th century invention—the moveable type press. German artists led the way in applying new techniques to fine prints. Wood printing blocks were too crude, so early engraving masters such as Martin Schöngauer and Albrecht Dürer made printing plates by making fine lines on a copper plate. In the 17th century, Rembrandt's etching technique was similar, except the artist drew onto a wax coating through which the copper plate was exposed to acid.

Traditional intaglio engravings have many common characteristics. An outline drawing is shaded with horizontal and diagonal lines, building up density by making the lines closer and by crosshatching and stippling. You can produce something similar in Photoshop by converting the image to Bitmap mode and using a halftone pattern—but unfortunately you'll find that the lines thicken where the image is darker. Instead, try using the Halftone Pattern filter.

This technique requires some practice, so start with a picture with clear lines and simple curves.

1 Use Ctrl/Cmd + J to duplicate the original image and convert it to black and white using Image > Adjustments > Desaturate. Copy the black and white layer and convert it to a line drawing using Filter > Stylize > Find Edges. Hide this layer by clicking the visibility eye.

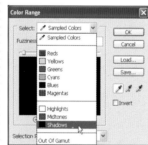

2 Hold down Alt/Opt and click the "Create a new layer" icon at the bottom of the Layers palette. Call the new layer "Shadows," set its blending mode to Multiply, and tick "Fill with Overlay-neutral color." Duplicate this layer (Ctrl/Cmd + J) and name the copy "Midtones."

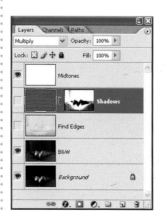

3 Choose Select > Color Range and pick Shadows from the drop-down box. Click OK. You should now see the selection's "marching ants."

4 With the Shadows layer active, click the "Add layer mask" icon in the Layers palette (the white circle inside the gray rectangle). This converts the selection into an image on the layer mask. Hide the Shadows layer.

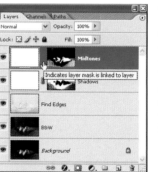

5 Activate the Midtones layer and repeat steps 3 and 4, this time selecting Midtones in the Color Range dialog box.

6 Make all your image layers visible, and click the chain between the Midtones layer thumbnail and its mask to unlink them. Do the same on the Shadows layer.

7 Make the foreground color white and the background color black (hit D, followed by X). On the Shadows layer, apply Filter > Sketch > Halftone Pattern. Make the Pattern Type Line, the Size small, and increase the contrast. Click OK.

8 Repeat step 7 for the Midtones layer.

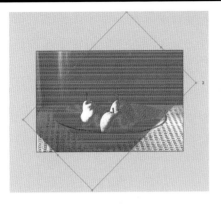

9 Ensure the Midtones layer is active, then zoom out a few times and pick **Edit > Free Transform**. Move the cursor to an area just outside the corner, wait for it to become a two-headed arrow, and rotate the layer roughly 45%.

10 Drag the sides of the layer and stretch it so it covers the entire image. Then double-click inside the box to apply the transformation.

11 It is possible that on some monitors the image will appear banded. Use Alt/Opt + Ctrl/Cmd + o to zoom to 100%. It will now consist of horizontal lines from the Shadows, diagonals from the Midtones, and the underlying Find Edges line drawing.

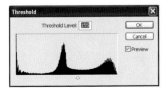

12 To remove the remaining shades from the Find Edges layer, add a Threshold adjustment layer. Move the slider beneath the histogram to get the balance right.

13 This completes the basic work, but you can also make the image look less mechanical. Hold down the Shift key and click the Midtones layer mask, switching the mask off. Reduce the layer's opacity and adjust the Threshold layer if needed. These steps will break up the diagonal lines.

14 Another possibility is to use **Edit > Free Transform** to stretch either the Midtones or the Shadows layers, dragging the lines further apart and making the image brighter. Again, you may have to fine-tune the Threshold layer.

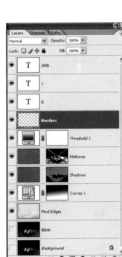

15 Use **Filter > Liquify** or **Edit > Transform > Warp** to curve the lines.

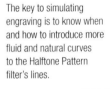

16 Other finishing touches include borders. I also added a signature, in the manner of Albrecht Dürer, who often signed and dated his prints.

The key to simulating engraving is to know when and how to introduce more fluid and natural curves to the Halftone Pattern filter's lines.

The Dutch portrait

In northern Europe, and especially in the Netherlands, many Calvinist patrons saw religious paintings as bordering on idolatry, and mistrusted the florid and extravagant Baroque style. Portrait painters such as Frans Hals and Rembrandt were commissioned by the wealthy merchants who dominated this society. Instead of dignifying the old aristocracy, they depicted patrons whose wealth came through hard work and virtue. The result was a less flattering, more natural style of portraiture.

The Dutch portrait style is informal, sometimes more like a candid photograph, and there is little theatricality. In Rembrandt's commissioned work as well as in his self-portraits, the subject is shown "warts and all," and the brushwork is much rougher than Baroque painters such as Rubens and Velázquez. The Dutch painters used a more sober color palette as well, often dominated by subdued shades of brown.

Look for informal, straightforward subjects. This man's face was full of character.

1 With the original image open, make the photograph black and white by adding a new Channel Mixer adjustment layer, ticking Monochrome and adjusting the channel sliders until you're satisfied with the result. Here I deliberately used more of the Blue channel because it's usually unkind to skin tones. This is a good start toward the look I'm aiming for.

2 Next, add a Curves adjustment layer to fine-tune the contrast. Here I first clicked the curve's midpoint (to preserve midtones), then dragged the shadows up and the highlights down. It's an adjustment layer, so you can fine-tune it later.

3 To add the base color, hold down the Alt/Opt key and click the "Create new fill or adjustment layer" icon. Give the layer an appropriate name and change the blending mode to Color. Click OK.

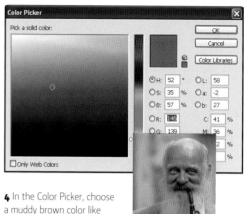

4 In the Color Picker, choose a muddy brown color like the one shown here and click OK.

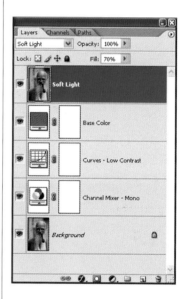

5 Duplicate the original image layer by dragging it down to the "Create a new layer" icon in the Layers palette. Then move it to the top of the layer stack, change its blending mode to Soft Light, and reduce its Fill Opacity to around 70%. This restores some of the original image color but also increases contrast.

6 Add another adjustment layer. It can be of any type, but don't change any of the settings. I chose Curves, but, since we're not making any changes, it hardly matters.

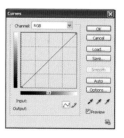

114

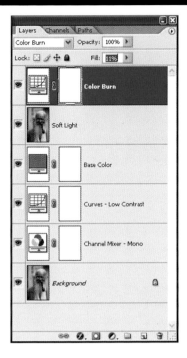

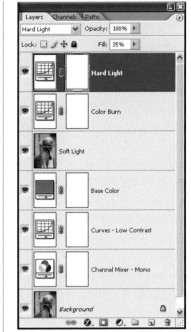

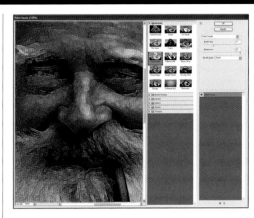

10 Apply the Artistic filter Paint Daubs to the merged layer. Leave the Brush type set to Simple and try various brush sizes. You are aiming at a fairly rustic result, so don't set the size too small. You will probably need to increase the sharpness as you increase the brush size.

7 In the Layers palette, change the new layer's blending mode and name to "Color Burn," and reduce the Fill Opacity to a low value. Small changes in this opacity setting make a big difference to the final result.

8 Repeat steps 6 and 7, but set the new adjustment layer's blending mode to Hard Light and its Fill Opacity to around 40%.

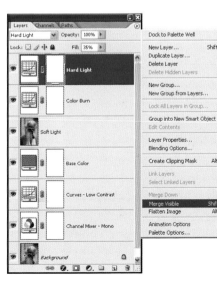

9 Fine-tune the various adjustment layers, then hold down the Alt/Opt key and bring up the Layers palette's menu by clicking the small black arrow. Select Merge Visible. This creates a new layer which you can use to add a painting effect.

17th-century Dutch portraits were much more naturalistic than their southern European counterparts, reflecting a certain Calvinist sobriety.

The Italian landscape

By the time of the Enlightenment in the 18th century, secular themes had become increasingly popular, even in southern Europe. Canaletto was the most famous Venetian painter of the era and worked mostly in Venice, but also in England. His images are luminous and meticulously detailed, thought to be the result of his use of a camera obscura—a darkened box or tent featuring a lens and mirrors that projected the intended subject of the painting onto a sheet of paper, allowing the draughtsman to trace the object.

Canaletto's paintings always seem rather dark. They show remarkably bright scenes with full sunlight bouncing off canals or rivers, but they appear a bit dull, with obvious cracks. It may be a deliberate tonal choice on the part of the artist, or that his soft colors just show the signs of aging more than earlier, darker paintings. Whatever the cause, these qualities can be imitated in Photoshop and are easy to apply to all types of "Old Masters."

This Las Vegas casino seemed a good substitute for Canaletto's Venice.

Why waste time creating artificial textures when you can just scan in a real one like this envelope, apply a Hue/Saturation or Levels adjustment, and then drag it into your image?

1 Open the original image. To add some clouds, hold down the Alt/Opt key and click the "Create a new layer" icon in the Layers palette. From the Mode drop-down menu, pick Lighten—anything painted on this layer will only be visible if it is lighter than the underlying image.

2 Set Photoshop's foreground color to a pale yellow that is noticeably lighter than the sky.

3 The background color should be a shade of blue similar to the sky, but a shade darker. Click the background color on Photoshop's Toolbar and use the Eyedropper to sample a pixel. Then, in the Color Picker, move the marker directly down.

4 Use the Lasso tool to make a cloud-shaped selection and soften its edges by pressing Alt/Opt + Ctrl/Cmd + D. In the Feather Selection dialog box, enter a radius of at least 20.

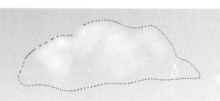

5 Go to **Filter** > **Render** > **Clouds** and review the result. If you don't like it, simply press Ctrl/Cmd + F to run the filter again.

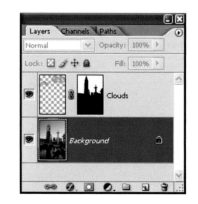

6 Feel free to allow clouds to go over a building, then create a layer mask for the Cloud layer. Temporarily switch back to the background layer, pick the Magic Wand tool and use it to select the sky, then activate the Clouds layer again and click the "Add layer mask" icon.

116

7 One way to add some aging cracks to the picture is to use the Craquelure filter. Hold the Alt/Opt and click the "Create a new layer" icon, this time with its blending mode set to Darken and with "Fill with Overlay-neutral Color" ticked.

8 Select an area to damage but don't feather the selection's edges. Reset Photoshop's foreground and background colors (shortcut D) and choose **Select > Texture > Craquelure** and experiment with the sliders.

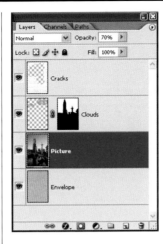

10 To give the painting an underlying texture, double-click the image layer so it is no longer a locked background, drag the envelope texture image (or other texture file) into the picture, and reduce the image layer's opacity.

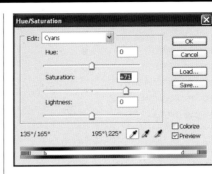

12 To color the picture in the style of Canaletto, add a Hue/Saturation adjustment layer. You should aim for strong yellows and cyans, so examine each color separately. Here I selected Cyan and increased its Saturation.

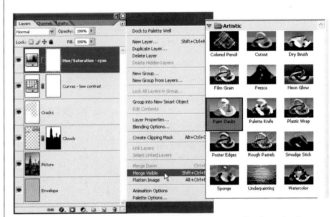

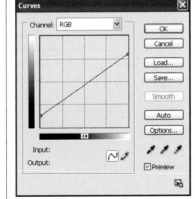

9 The crack effect is probably too strong, so reduce the layer's opacity. Other ways to make it less regular are to use the Eraser tool randomly, or distort it with **Filter > Distort > Wave**, or **Edit > Transform > Warp**.

11 At the top of the layer stack, add a new Curves adjustment layer to reduce the picture's contrast. Drag the bottom-left point up a little so there won't be true blacks in the picture, and drag the top-right point down to take out the highlights.

13 Finally, make the image look more like a painting. First, merge the layers, holding down the Alt/Opt key, clicking the small black arrow at the top of the Layers palette, and selecting Merge Visible from the drop-down menu. Then apply **Filter > Artistic > Paint Daubs**. Don't use settings that are too high, unless you want the picture to appear Impressionistic. A small brush size combined with a higher Sharpness setting works best.

This Las Vegas casino will probably be demolished and replaced before it has time to grow old, but aging this photograph is easy in Photoshop.

The 18th-century vignette

B y the late 18th century, portrait painting had moved on from Rembrandt's unsentimental, natural treatment. Sir Joshua Reynolds, the leading English portrait artist, believed in dignity but introduced a softer, more decorative style.

Today it's easier than ever to carry pictures of loved ones around with us. Perhaps in the future people will have a sentimental view of how we display them on mobile phones and other devices. Or maybe lockets and small picture frames are here to stay. So, how might one go about simulating such a locket after the style of Reynolds or another 18th-century portrait artist?

In this example, I'll use adjustment layers and layer styles to simulate just this look. A solid color will be linked to the picture to adjust the tone, and a textured shape will be blended with the image to simulate glass. Finally, Photoshop's Styles palette provides a wide variety of possible frame textures.

This technique works well with any image that has one overwhelming color cast, or where the photographer has used flashes of color, so choose your photo accordingly.

1 With the image open, add a new layer by clicking in the Layers palette, click the "Create new fill or adjustment layer" icon and select Solid Color. In the resulting Color Picker dialog box, select the color you want. I wanted to add a chocolate brown.

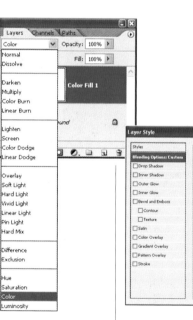

2 Still in the Layers palette, change the blending mode of the Solid Color layer to Color. This lets the original picture show through, and accents it with the fill color we've chosen.

3 Right/Ctrl-click the Solid Color layer and select Blending Options. Select your accent color from the Blend If drop-down menu at the bottom of the Layer Style dialog.

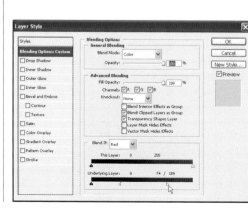

4 Drag the Underlying Layer slider's white triangle. As you move the triangle, the accent color starts to show through the Solid Color layer. What is happening is that Photoshop is showing the underlying pixels if the Red channel value is over 121. Another way to think of it is that it is only showing the current layer's brown pixels if the Red channel in the underlying layer is a low value—between 0 and 121.

5 At the moment the transition is not very subtle, but this is easy to fix. Hold down the Alt/Opt key, drag one half of the white triangle away from the other, and adjust them independently.

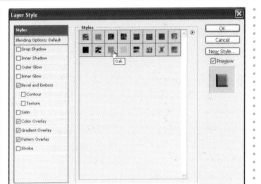

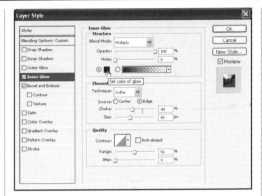

6 To add the vignette window, add a new layer and set the foreground color to white. Then select Custom Shapes from the Toolbar, select an appropriate shape from the Options Bar, and set its options to Fill Pixels, allowing a large enough radius for the image.

10 Tick Inner Glow, and make the glow's color match the image; try out other settings if you wish. Then click OK.

14 As a final step, I decided to crop the girl more tightly and held down Shift as I used Edit > Free Transform on the layer. Then I added a frame, copied the Glass layer, stretched it and chose a preset style from the Blending Options. Because all the key elements are in layers, you're free to fine-tune the results.

7 Create a new blank layer and call it "Glass." Click and drag across the image and Photoshop will paint your shape onto a new layer.

8 In the Layers palette, reduce the layer's Fill Opacity percentage to 0, click the "Add a layer style" icon, and select Bevel and Emboss.

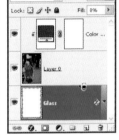

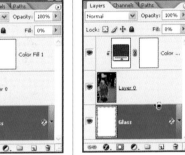

11 To complete the basic vignette, move the Glass layer to the bottom of the layer stack. If there is a locked background layer, hold down the Alt/Opt key and double-click it.

12 Hold down the Alt/Opt key and click the line between each layer. The layer above will appear indented in the Layers palette and will only affect the one directly below it.

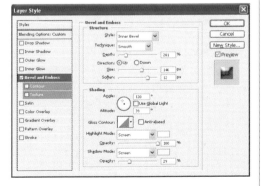

9 The main settings to change are Size and Soften, which need to be high. Also adjust the Angle—you can drag the crosshairs around the circle's edge and inside, too.

13 Also try an Artistic or Brush Strokes filter to make the picture look more like a painting. The Paint Daubs filter worked well here—notice that I zoomed in to 100% to see the effect on the girl's face.

A vignette with a difference—simulating a locket's glass cover. Vignettes were traditionally oval in shape, but feel free to choose a shape that suits the subject.

119

The luminous landscape

J.M.W. Turner was probably the most adventurous painter of the first half of the 19th century, creating landscapes of astonishing abstraction. Echoing the earlier French painter Claude Lorrain, Turner evoked the brightness of Mediterranean light but in such dazzling, luminous swirls that his Italian landscapes, images of Venice, and classical themes were sometimes barely recognizable. Stormy northern oceans became frothing torrents of waves and spray, while steam trains rushed through billowing smoke. What Turner conveyed was the *impression* of what we know the scene contains, and he did so over 50 years before the Impressionists.

A swirling luminosity is the most obvious characteristic of Turner's style, and it was used to evoke both the brilliance of warm sun and the violence of the sea. To give a photograph such a feeling, begin by intensifying certain colors—pale blues and rich yellow tones for a sunny day, or cold grays and blues for bad weather. Next, create a layer of clouds, and swirl and distort it, making it either subtle and radiant or powerful and stormy.

Turner traveled widely—especially in Italy—and coastal scenes are particularly appropriate for this treatment. Cities with rivers and bridges were also favorite subjects.

1 Open your selected image, add a new layer, and set its blending mode to Hard Light. This layer will hold the artificial sun, so name it "Sun."

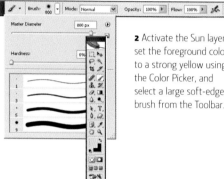

2 Activate the Sun layer, set the foreground color to a strong yellow using the Color Picker, and select a large soft-edged brush from the Toolbar.

3 Add the misty sun with a single dab of the brush.

4 To depict the sun's white-hot center, reduce the brush size and set the Brush tool's blending mode to Screen. Dab again inside the sun, just below its center. Reduce the brush size again, and dab again until the central brightness is almost white. It's probably better if the dabs are not all in exactly the same spot.

5 To enhance the sun's glow, click the "Add a layer style" icon in the Layer palette and choose Outer Glow. In the Layer Styles dialog box, change the blending mode to Multiply or Color Burn, and the glow's color to yellow. You may also want to reduce the layer style's opacity.

6 Create another layer with hard Light blending beneath your Sun and call it "Sky". Click the "Add layer mask" icon for the Sky layer and, with the mask active, select the Gradient tool and choose Linear Gradient in the Tool Options Bar. The foreground color should now be white and the background black. Next, hold Shift and drag from roughly where you placed the sun down to just below the horizon.

7 Click the Sky layer's image thumbnail, and ensure the Gradient tool is still selected. Set Photoshop's foreground color to a pale blue (such as RGB values 165 178 255) and the background to a rich yellow (255 240 100).

8 Drag downward and fill the Sky layer with the blue-to-yellow gradient. If you don't like the result, simply drag over it again.

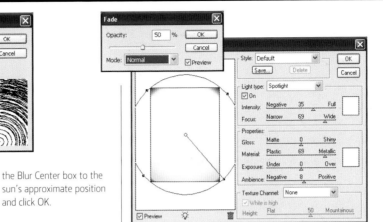

14 For a subtle, painterly effect, apply the Lighting Effects filter to the Sky layer (**Filter** > **Render** > **Lighting Effects**). Immediately afterward, use **Edit** > **Fade Lighting Effects** to fine-tune its impact.

9 Because the Sun and Sky are in layers, you can fine-tune the results. If the colors are too strong, change the opacity of either layer or adjust the Sun's layer style. Here I reduced the Sun layer's opacity just a little. If the effect is too weak, duplicate a layer or experiment with the blending modes.

11 Without releasing the selection, choose **Filter** > **Blur** > **Radial Blur**. Drag the Blur Center box to the sun's approximate position and click OK.

15 Finally, add a Photo Filter adjustment layer. I closed my selection and then added a warming filter, which unified the picture with its overall color cast.

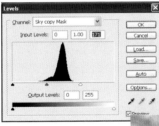

12 The Radial Blur filter can make the sky's colors almost disappear if you apply it to the mask. After all, it blurs the black-and-white cloud shapes and makes the mask gray. To fix this, using the same selection, hit Ctrl/Cmd + L to adjust the Levels. Drag the white and gray triangles to the left to reveal the now-swirling clouds.

121

10 Next, add some swirling clouds. Ctrl/Cmd-Click the Sky layer's mask so Photoshop creates a selection. Then go to **Filter** > **Render** > **Clouds**. For a stronger stormy effect, apply it to the Sky layer. In this case, the landscape needs a gentler effect, so activate the layer's mask by clicking it without holding down the Ctrl/Cmd key, and then apply the Clouds filter.

13 If you are using Photoshop CS2, you may want to stretch the selection with the new Warp transformation tool, which is found under **Edit** >**Transform**. Here I just dragged one of the Warp box's lines upward and spread the sun's radiance over the whole frame.

Creating a soft, restrained atmosphere is probably harder than adding so much swirling chaos that the picture becomes totally unrecognizable. Adding the atmosphere on separate layers means you can reuse it with other suitable photographs.

The Romantic landscape

Nineteenth-century Romanticism was a loose movement spanning many of the arts. In painting, it exalted the beauty of nature—particularly wild landscapes—and used it to inject feeling and significance. Thomas Cole and the Hudson River School showed the northeast United States as grand and inspiring, while in Germany, Caspar David Friedrich showed bleak and mountainous landscapes that somehow conveyed a feeling of hope.

Simulating snow or rain is often a lot easier than being out there with your camera, and can completely change the picture's atmosphere and mood.

If the snow had been falling, I probably wouldn't have been out with my camera at this Wuthering Heights-style building.

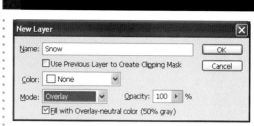

1 Open your image, and in the Layers palette, hold down Alt/Opt and click the "Add a new layer" icon. Call the new layer "Snow," set its blending mode to Overlay, and tick "Fill with Overlay-neutral color."

3 Apply a little Gaussian blur—enough to make the Snow layer's grains form into clumps.

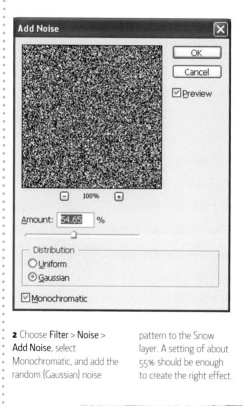

2 Choose **Filter** > **Noise** > **Add Noise**, select Monochromatic, and add the random (Gaussian) noise pattern to the Snow layer. A setting of about 55% should be enough to create the right effect.

4 Activate the Levels adjustment with Ctrl/Cmd + L and drag the dialog's white and black sliders until the snowdrops turn white.

5 Change the Snow layer's blending mode to Lighten. Optionally, apply some Motion Blur to make the snow appear as though it's falling.

7 Make two or three similar layers, but vary the settings. You want the snow to look more three-dimensional, so make it smaller and more blurred. Here I made some snowflakes appear closer by using **Edit > Free Transform** (Ctrl/Cmd + T) to stretch the new layer.

8 To give the impression of gusting wind, apply **Edit > Transform > Warp** to some of the snow layers. This displays a grid with lines you can drag at will. Use different warps for different snow layers.

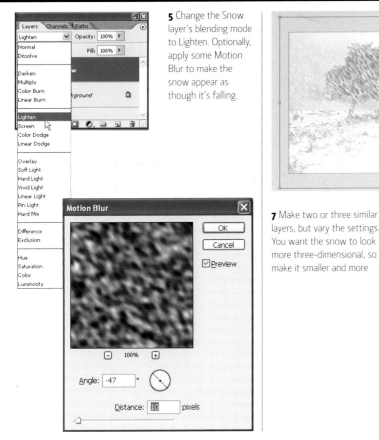

6 Fine-tune the effect with another Levels adjustment, or add more Gaussian blur.

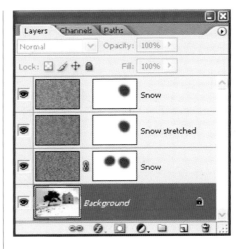

9 Don't worry too much if some key details are obscured by snow. Add layer masks and use a soft-edged brush to paint a shade of gray onto the mask. The darker the shade, the less dense that layer's snow will appear.

Romanticism was about finding meaning or symbolism in the landscape. This isolated house now offers shelter from the driving snow.

Japanese printmaking

In 1856, Japan was forced to open its ports to trade, and Japanese woodcut prints suddenly became available in America and Europe. The work of artists such as Hokusai, Utamaro, and Hiroshige was well-known by the Impressionists and was very influential—Japanese prints appear in works by Manet, van Gogh, and Gauguin. But the fascination was not one-way. Japanese printmaking had grown in isolation, with occasional infusions of Chinese styles, but Hokusai and his colleagues had also studied European landscape painting. Their prints dispensed with traditional scenes and were more like Western-style landscapes seen through Japanese eyes.

Nineteenth-century Japanese prints often used a pigment called Prussian Blue, and rarely contain more than four colors in a print. There is little tonal gradation. Shapes are outlined, often in blue. The most famous artist, Hokusai, produced many rural and coastal landscapes but is best-known for a series of prints, *Thirty-six Views of Mount Fuji*, which included his *Great Wave of Kanagawa*. For many people, Mount Fuji symbolizes Japan. Luckily, it's not too difficult to draw its perfect shape.

If you have no images of Mount Fuji, use something else that may be appropriate. Start with a black-and-white picture such as this wave from South Africa.

124

1 Open your image. In the Layers palette, click the "Create new fill or adjustment layer" icon and select Color Balance. Add the blue tone to the Shadows, dragging the top slider toward Cyan, and the bottom one toward Blue.

2 On another Color Balance adjustment layer, make the Highlights a sepia color.

3 Right/Ctrl-click the Color Balance sepia layer and select Blending Options. Drag Blend If's black triangle to the right, so that the blue color shows through. To smooth the blue-sepia transition, hold down the Alt/Opt key and drag half of the black triangle.

4 To add the edges, copy the background layer, switch the new layer's blending mode to Multiply, then apply the Find Edges filter using **Filter > Stylize > Find Edges**.

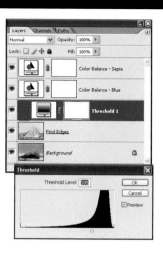

5 A Threshold adjustment layer can make the Find Edges layer more like a line drawing. To ensure it only affects the Find Edges layer, hold down the Alt/Opt key and click the line between the two layers.

6 To draw the volcano, first create a path with the Pen tool. Be sure that its options are set to Path, then click once where you want the volcano's left slope to start, hold down Shift, and click again where you want its right slope to end. You should now have a line with handles at each end.

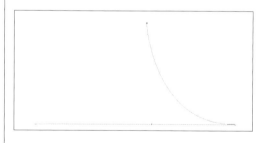

7 Drag the mouse back along the line until it is near the middle. Release the mouse button and click once where you want the summit. Photoshop will draw the right-hand slope.

8 To make the volcano's mouth, drag again for a short distance to the left and slightly downward. Release the mouse button and click where the other side of the mouth should be. This will draw a curve across the summit.

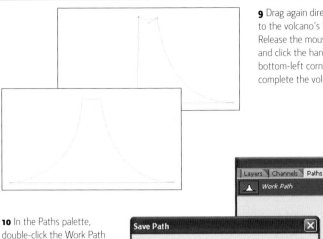

9 Drag again directly down to the volcano's baseline. Release the mouse button and click the handle at the bottom-left corner to complete the volcano.

10 In the Paths palette, double-click the Work Path and name it "Fuji."

11 You can fine-tune the path using the Direct Selection tool. Click the left slope to make the handle visible, and drag it to the left to make the slope less steep.

12 When the volcano shape is correct, Ctrl/Cmd-click the Fuji path in the Paths palette, so that the volcano shape becomes a marching ants selection. Add a new layer (Ctrl/Cmd + Shift + N) and immediately click the "Add layer mask" icon—your selection should now become a volcano-shaped mask.

13 Paint freely on the Volcano layer. Use the Gradient tool, dragging it upward. To make sure the volcano picks up the blues and sepias, keep its layer below the two Color Balance layers. (Hokusai depicted Fuji in all seasons and used various colors, even an ochre red, so move the layer to the top of the stack if you want to apply other colors.) Use the Multiply blending mode on the Volcano layer.

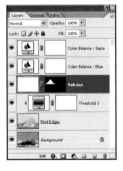

14 Don't forget to add an outline to the volcano. Select its area by holding down Ctrl/Cmd and clicking the mask, then choose **Edit > Stroke** and use blue or black. Use the Eraser tool to wash away the volcano's lower slopes and paint some white streaks of snow at the summit.

15 Hokusai often made Fuji a small but still important element of his compositions. To change the volcano's size, ensure no selection is active and then use **Edit > Free Transform** to resize the whole layer.

16 A finishing touch is to add a wordy title. Rather than pretend to write Japanese (unless you do!), add text in a column and then put a shape layer below it. (To type into a column, select the Type tool as usual, but rather than clicking where you wish to start typing, click and drag to form a box to enclose your text.) Again, use the Multiply blending mode so the shape becomes part of the print.

This volcano was drawn using the Pen tool. This is great for creating stylized shapes or "paths." You can then drag the path to other pictures, fine-tune it, and create a series of views of Mount Fuji.

The Impressionist landscape

Though soon to be a badge of pride for painters such as Monet, Manet, Renoir, and Pisarro, the term "Impressionism" was originally how one critic dismissed the work of this group of 19th-century, Paris-based artists. Dissatisfied with studio-perfected representations of scenes, these painters sought to record what their eyes had actually seen. This often involved painting on the spot, brushing colors rapidly onto the canvas and capturing their overall impressions of a scene. The critic's ridicule was short-lived, and Impressionism has proved to be one of the most enduring and popular artistic movements.

Many of the Impressionists had spent time in London and were familiar with the works of the English painter, J. M. W. Turner; like Turner, their landscape paintings were also exercises in conveying the impression of light and atmosphere. Often the appearance is blurred, foggy, and degraded, and the minute details of a photograph are absent. So, emulating this in Photoshop is a matter of applying filters and emphasizing the direction and character of the light. But the key is to convey the atmosphere of the location depicted.

This was as close as I could get to Monet's view of London's Houses of Parliament.

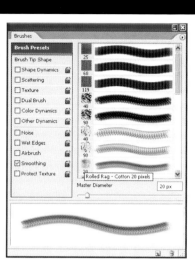

1 After opening the image, you first need to create a new lighting source. Click the "Create a new layer" icon in the Layers palette, and name it "Sun."

2 Select a large, soft-edged brush via the Toolbar and choose an appropriate color for the sun's outer glow. Dab once or twice with the brush. Repeat this a few times, reducing the brush size and subtly changing the color. Do the same for the reflection.

3 In the Layers palette, hold down Alt/Opt and click the "Add a new layer" icon. Set its blending mode to Overlay and tick "Fill with Overlay–neutral color." This will be the cloud layer.

4 To make the clouds, choose one of the more irregular brush shapes. There are some interesting ones in the Faux Finish and Natural Media presets that are available under the Brush's Presets menu.

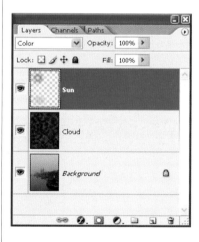

5 Use a large, soft, brush shape and stipple the Overlay layer with a darker shade. Don't worry about the precise color; the color's luminosity is what matters. Here I painted with shades of gray.

6 Now we need to apply a layer style to the whole layer which will give the image texture and tone. Click the Layers palette's "Add a layer style" icon and choose Color Overlay.

7 In the Layer Style dialog box, set the Blend Mode to Color, choose a rich blue color, and reduce its opacity to around 60%.

8 Now, add a Pattern Overlay. The Light Marble pattern from Photoshop's Rock Patterns set creates a perfect look. Set the scale to 1000%, opacity to 48%, and the blend mode to Luminosity.

9 Go to **File** > **Save As...** to save a layered copy of the file under a different name, in case you wish to make changes later. Then, on the original file, select the top layer in the Layers stack, hold down the Alt/Opt key, and choose Merge Visible from the Layers palette menu.

10 With the image now on a single layer, you can apply a variety of filters. But instead of applying them to the entire layer, make a selection first. This approach works really well with filters such as Sprayed Strokes that allow you to specify an angle. Here I wanted the water to be "painted" in a different direction than the rest of the picture.

11 A sharp-edged selection would probably be too obvious in the final image. You can use **Select** > **Feather** and enter a selection-softening radius, or you can take the guesswork out of it by switching into the Quick Mask mode by pressing Q and then applying the Gaussian Blur filter. Ensure that Preview is ticked, then adjust the Radius slider. When the edge looks right, click OK, then press Q again to return to standard mode.

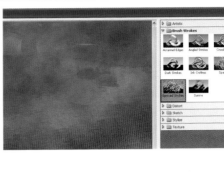

12 The Sprayed Strokes filter can give a pleasing Impressionist effect. Here I increased the Size and Radius, making the effect more obvious; and Horizontal is the water's most suitable Direction setting for water, because the ripples seem natural.

13 Now, select the rest of the picture, using Ctrl/Cmd + Shift + I to invert the selection, and click Alt/Opt + Ctrl/Cmd + F to apply the same filter, this time with more restrained settings.

14 Finally, a filter should be applied to the whole image for a consistent feel. Here I applied **Filter** > **Artistic** > **Paint Daubs**. Low settings added nice edges to some of the distinctive shapes.

Modern London, looking much as it might have through Monet's eyes, save perhaps for Millbank Tower peeping out from behind the Houses of Parliament.

Seurat and the Pointillists

Georges Seurat was one of the leading exponents of the Neo-Impressionist movement of the late 19th century. He is most famous for developing a technique known as "Pointillism," a style of painting that utilized small colored dots or brush strokes. The resulting mosaic of pure color looks more luminous than if it had been composed of brush strokes of blended colors. Some of the major Pointillist works contained millions of dots, so the technique was very laborious. However, creating your own Pointillist-inspired piece is easy in Photoshop, because the program includes a Pointillist filter that breaks up the colors in an image into dots and uses the background color to fill in the areas of canvas between them.

Because their paintings were composed only of dots—no lines or edges—the Pointillists needed to simplify forms. The same applies in Photoshop, so you need to choose an original image with strong shapes and blocks of color. Faces lose much of their detail, and Seurat often chose to paint people staring blankly across a scene. Another feature of many of his paintings is a dark border area made up of restrained colors (often gray) that were consistent with the rest of the image.

Seurat is best known for scenes by lakes, rivers, harbors, and coastlines, but applying a basic Pointillist effect in Photoshop is so simple that you can experiment freely with other subjects. I've chosen a photograph of the Golden Gate Bridge.

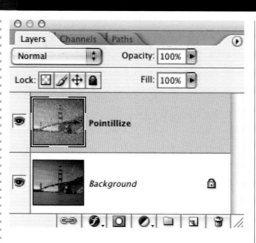

1 It's always best to leave the original image untouched so, in the Layers palette, copy the image layer by dragging it to the "Create a new layer" icon or by using Ctrl/Cmd + J. Name the layer "Pointillize."

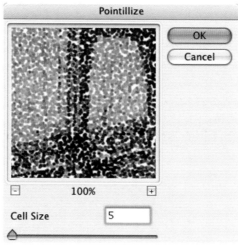

2 Now you're ready to "pointillize" the picture. Set the background color to white so that when you use the Pointillize filter the background canvas between the dots will remain white.

Select **Filter > Pixellate > Pointillize** and set a low Cell Size value. This image is about 1600 pixels wide, and a Cell Size of 5 retains enough detail.

3 Review the filter's results by zooming the image to 100% or Actual Pixels using Alt/Opt + Ctrl/Cmd + 0. If you need to undo the filter, use Ctrl/Cmd + Z, and then re-open the Pointillize filter dialog with Alt/Opt + Ctrl/Cmd + F, to see whether a different Cell Size value is more effective.

Tip

PIXEL PREVIEW

While you are using filters, Photoshop will display a preview image whether the zoom percentage is 100% or not. Especially with pixelated or noisy images, the preview can be misleading at anything other than 100%, which is why many filters also have a smaller preview within their own dialog boxes.

Fade

Opacity: 90 %

Mode: Screen

OK
Cancel
☑ Preview

4 Use **Edit** > **Fade**, which is only available immediately after you apply the Pointillize filter. Drag the slider to reduce the filter's effect and change the mode to Screen.

The result is similar to changing the Pointillize layer's blending mode. Keep in mind, however, that you can't fine-tune a Fade later.

Curves

Channel: RGB

OK
Cancel
Load...
Save...
Smooth
Auto
Options...

Input: 95
Output: 158

☑ Preview

5 To recreate the subdued look of Pointillist paintings, click the "Create new fill or adjustment layer" icon and select Curves. Drag the curve upward to lighten the colors. Alternatively, you could try changing the blending mode to Screen, but Curves gives you more precise control.

6 To create a dark border around the picture, use the Polygonal Lasso tool to make a rough rectangular selection a few pixels in from the image edge—it doesn't matter if it's quite crude.

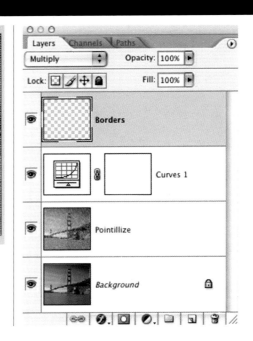

Layers | Channels | Paths

Multiply Opacity: 100%

Lock: Fill: 100%

Borders

Curves 1

Pointillize

Background

7 Invert the selection (Ctrl/ Cmd + Shift + I) so that only the edges are selected. Use Ctrl/Cmd + J to copy the selection onto a new layer, name the layer "Borders," and drag it to the top of the layer stack. Providing it's darker than the rest of the picture, what you do with the Borders layer is up to you. Blur it and apply the Pointillize filter again, desaturate it, or use **Image** > **Adjustments** > **Brightness/Contrast**. Seurat explored various styles.

This image works well with the Pointillist filter. Much of the detail in the bridge has disappeared, but its red paint survives as strong vertical and horizontal shapes, and the coastal location and blue tones seem appropriate. Who cares if the Golden Gate Bridge wasn't built until half a century after Pointillism?

Van Gogh's Sunflowers

In the late 1880s, Dutch painter Vincent Van Gogh created his most famous works in a brief period while living in Arles, in southern France. These included Provençal landscapes, indoor scenes, and vases of sunflowers.

Influenced by Impressionism and Post-Impressionism, as well as by Japanese art, Van Gogh's style is distinct and instantly recognizable. His work is characterized by thick swirls of solid color, as can be seen in many of his skies, but he also painted poplar trees and fields of waving crops. In his sunflower paintings, Van Gogh limited his palette to golds, mustards, and contrasting blues, and he tended to compose the images within tight framing in order to focus the eye. The thick swirls form a backdrop for the slightly scruffy, withered petals of his flowers, outlined in prominent black lines.

130

My local flower store only had fresh sunflowers, nothing as old or wilted as van Gogh's subjects, but I emulated the style of the painting by making one stem droop away from the bunch. I placed the vase on a

low table against a simple, contrasting background that would be easy to remove digitally. Using a short zoom lens, I used an angle of view similar to van Gogh's for a striking composition.

1 To create a contrasting background, select and remove the existing background with the Magic Wand. Set a low tolerance and click a pixel typical of the area. Hold down Shift to add other pixels (or Alt/Opt to subtract them) from the selection.

2 When the selection looks correct, click the "Add a new layer" icon in the Layers palette and immediately click the new layer's "Add

layer mask" icon. This layer will be used for painting a new swirling background; the mask will protect the sunflowers underneath.

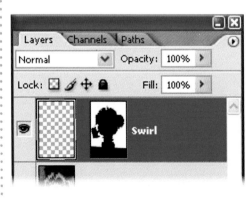

3 Click the chain between the thumbnail and the mask to unlink them. This stops later steps from affecting the mask.

4 Set the foreground color to turquoise, mustard, or a deep shade of blue, and fill the layer with **Edit > Fill**. Use the Brush tool to paint onto the layer, but use a slightly different shade of the same color. There is no need for artistic skill—random strokes will be fine.

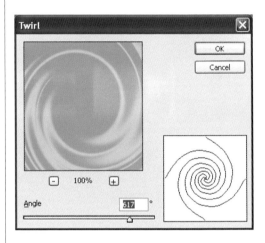

5 Choose the Marquee tool (shortcut M) and select an area—the smaller the area, the tighter the swirls will be. From Photoshop's Filters menu, select **Distort**

> **Twirl**. As you drag the Angle slider, you see a preview of how Photoshop will twirl the selection. When you are happy with the result, click OK.

6 Make a new selection and apply the Twirl filter again. Here, I have already applied the filter to areas above the flowers and to their right, and have moved the selection marquee, ready for another twirl. Repeat this process until every

part of the background has been affected. Save time by using Ctrl/Cmd + F, which reapplies the same filter settings, or use Alt/Opt + Ctrl/Cmd + F to reopen the dialog box and change the angle.

7 If your vase and tabletop are as unsuitable as mine, activate the Magic Lasso, zoom in, and select them by dragging around them. Use Ctrl/Cmd + J to copy them into their own layers.

8 With these elements in separate layers, you can safely experiment. Paint randomly with the brush, or choose **Filter > Filter Gallery**, click the "New effect layer" icon at the bottom right of the dialog, and apply multiple filters simultaneously. Here, Poster Edges was perfect for creating cracks on this vase, while Paint Daubs smudged the colors.

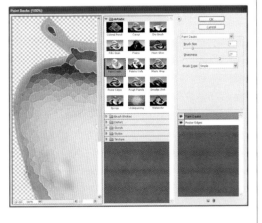

9 Van Gogh's vase had a line halfway across, so I selected the top of my vase and added a strong border using **Edit > Stroke**. I also used **Image > Adjustments > Hue/Saturation** to fine-tune the color, then used other settings on its lower half. The top was gold, the base beige.

10 Van Gogh usually gave every detail an edge. As all the image elements are on different layers, it's easier to merge them onto a new layer before proceeding. Hold down the Alt/Opt key and select Merge Visible from the Layers palette menu (if you are using Photoshop CS or earlier versions of Photoshop, you should first create a new layer). Then select **Filter > Artistic > Poster Edges**. Turn the Posterize slider down, and adjust the edges to match the image. I used low values.

For a final touch, place your signature in the same position on the vase as Van Gogh did on the original sunflower paintings.

131

Nocturnes

Impressionism attracted numerous artists to the streets of Paris. American painter James McNeill Whistler was there at the start, exhibiting alongside the Impressionists in the Salon of 1863. Whistler also admired Turner's atmospheric work and particularly shared his interest in Japanese art. What made Whistler unique was that he painted nighttime scenes—now known as the "Nocturnes."

Whistler was drawn to the River Thames in London and painted jetties and bridges, often at night and cloaked in mist. These subjects signal the Japanese influence on the Nocturnes, in addition to the use of block-like structures of verticals and horizontals. Another key feature is the subdued palette of cool blues, grays, and blacks.

I've always felt the jetty in this image had a slightly Japanese atmosphere. It was taken on a pretty, gray afternoon.

1 Open the image and use Ctrl/Cmd + Alt/Opt + J to copy the image layer, switching its blending mode to Multiply. This immediately darkens the whole image, rather like the results of underexposing the picture in-camera. Repeat, creating more layers, until the image is dark enough. Save on disk space by merging these "Night for Day" layers.

2 If the Night for Day layer makes the shadows so dark they lose something of their detail, right/Ctrl-click the layer in the Layers palette and choose Blending Options.

3 In the Layer Style dialog box, go to the Blend If section and drag the This Layer slider's black triangle to the right. This hides the darker shades on the Night for Day layer.

4 While this improves the shadows, there is an unfortunate transitional effect—you can see it along the post in step 3. To resolve this, hold down the Alt/Opt key and drag at one side of the Blend If black triangle. The triangle splits in two, and you can adjust the two halves to produce a smooth transition.

132

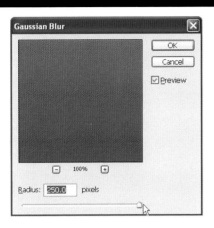

5 To add a bit of nocturnal gloom, use **Filter > Blur > Gaussian Blur**. Lower radius values may cause a halo around some features, so use a higher value for this effect.

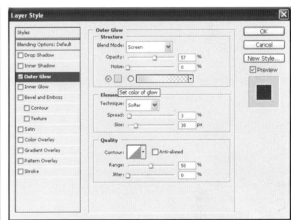

8 For extra darkening, create a new layer, and set its blending mode to Overlay. Use the Gradient tool to add shading from the top of the posts up to the sky.

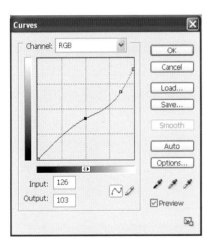

6 Fine-tune the image with a Curves adjustment layer. To retain the tone in important areas, such as the jetty shadows, click two or three times on the curve before you start dragging it. Here, the two higher points were dragged downward to darken highlights. Photoshop automatically moved the lower-left point down, too, so I had to drag it back up. The result—a reversed S-shape—held shadow detail in the jetty while darkening the sky and clouds.

9 Whistler's scenes often include the glow of distant streetlights. To emulate this effect, paint them on a new layer (Ctrl/Cmd + Shift + N). Select a small, hard-edged Brush tool. Paint just a few yellow dots—here, a series of lights were painted along a road weaving down to the river bank.

10 While a soft-edged brush would be perfect for simulating the glow of the streetlights, it is better to use the Layer Style, which you can fine-tune much more easily. Click the "Add a layer style" icon in the Layers palette and select Outer Glow. Set the color to yellow and adjust the size until you achieve the desired effect.

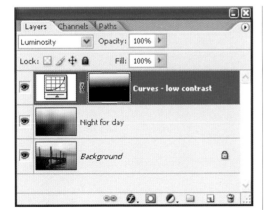

7 To fine-tune the effect of the Curves adjustment layer, paint on its layer mask. Painting with black eliminates the effect, while white applies it at full strength.

The subdued "night for day" effects employed here retain interesting detail in the shadow areas.

Fauve scenes

"Les Fauves"—meaning savages or wild beasts—were a group of young painters that made its name after exhibiting in Paris in 1905. Loosely characterized by a disregard for the natural representation of color, the Fauves sought to be expressive and bold. Matisse was a leading advocate and inspirational figure for the group, but others associated with it included Raoul Dufy, André Derain, and American painters such as Alfred Maurer and Anne Estelle Rice.

Probably the most accessible Fauvist style to recreate in Photoshop is that of Dufy. Typically depicting sunny coastal views, harbors, and bays with yachts and palm trees, Dufy's paintings favored pastel colors, especially pale blues and pinks. Shapes were roughly outlined and the colors washed over the lines, producing a combination of line and color that rather resembles colored tracing paper or imperfect registration.

Look for colorful images with lots of strong detail, like the trees and railings in this Mediterranean scene.

1 Open the image and duplicate the image layer. Use Alt/Opt + Ctrl/Cmd + J and name the layer "Edges."

2 Convert the Edges layer to a line drawing using **Filter > Stylize > Find Edges**.

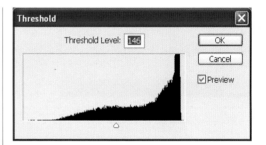

3 In the Layers palette, click the "Create new fill or adjustment layer" icon and select Threshold. Drag the slider until all the color disappears.

Tip

POSTER EDGES

An alternative way to create a line-drawing effect is to use the Poster Edges filter (Filter > Artistic > Poster Edges). This option gives you more flexibility, and can produce stronger lines. However, it can also result in very black shadows, which may not be appropriate for all images.

4 If the line drawing shows fine details, such as the leaves and litter in the foreground, apply a small amount of Gaussian Blur to the Edges layer. A radius of 1 was enough to clean up this picture.

7 Activate the Move tool (shortcut V), hold down Shift and use one of the arrow keys to nudge the Multiply layer a few pixels in one direction. The effect you are looking for is a slight mismatch between the colors and the black lines, as though the registration of the image is slightly off.

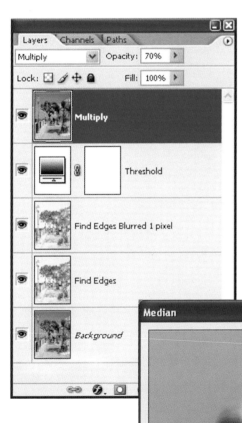

5 When the line drawing looks right, duplicate the original image layer again (Ctrl/Cmd + J). Drag the new layer to the top of the layer stack, switch its blending mode to Multiply, and reduce its opacity a little. The image now looks like a line drawing that has been colored in.

The Fauves were a loosely associated group of painters including Henri Matisse, André Derain, and Raoul Dufy. Their work was controversial at the time for its bold use of color and painting styles.

135

6 Apply the Median filter to the new Multiply layer. This filter is found under **Filter > Noise** and it blends neighboring pixels within the radius. Set a high enough radius that the image is barely recognizable in the Preview—this shows the top of a man's head.

Klimt and Art Nouveau

Art Nouveau was an international style at the turn of the 20th century that combined function with richly decorative form. Hector Guimard's Paris Metro entrances are typical, both in their urban location and their fluid, cast-iron curves and lettering. A Japanese influence can be seen on Toulouse Lautrec's posters and Charles Rennie Mackintosh's rectilinear furniture. Celtic tradition and natural forms can be seen in Louis Sullivan's Chicago skyscrapers, and, in New York, the glassware of Louis Comfort Tiffany echoed Medieval and Islamic art. In Austria, the style was known as Secessionstil; its eclectic influence can best be seen in the major works of Gustav Klimt.

Some of Klimt's best-known paintings showed embracing couples, or women wrapped in enormous garments. Gold leaf was used extensively—emulating religious icons—and the canvas was filled with extravagant patterns reminiscent of Arabic, Persian, and Turkish styles. Imitating the style in Photoshop involves simulating the gold—for which many recipes are available—and creating a range of custom brush shapes, which you can use to paint the patterns.

Any portrait can be used—most of the work is in creating the gold leaf and the patterns.

1 After opening the image, create the gold leaf background. Click the "Create a new layer" icon in the Layers palette and set Photoshop's foreground and background colors to two shades of brown—try RGB values 113 90 56 and 180 160 107. Select **Filter > Render > Clouds**. This produces cloud patterns with the foreground and background colors.

2 For a gentle brushed effect, choose **Filter > Noise > Add Noise**. Tick Gaussian and Monochrome and set a small amount. Then apply some blur using **Filter > Blur > Motion Blur** and set a low Distance value.

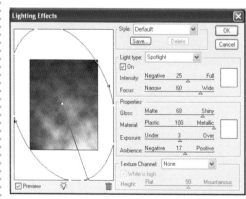

3 Apply some directional light using **Filter > Render > Lighting Effects**. You can drag the preview circle's handles or use the sliders. By setting the Focus slider to a high value, the glow is nicely diffused. If the effect is too strong, **Edit > Fade Lighting Effects** acts as a partial Undo, but you must apply it immediately.

4 To flake the gold leaf, choose **Filter > Artistic > Paint Daubs** and push the sharpness to a high setting. If this produces unpleasant color noise, select **Edit > Fade Paint Daubs** and switch the blending mode to Luminosity.

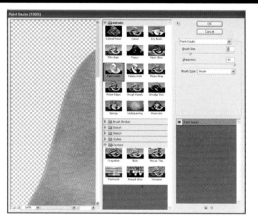

5 Klimt showed his figures on a base of flowers, so add a new layer, call it "Base," and select the Brush tool. Make its size large (]) and its edges hard (Shift +]). Then paint with any color.

6 To fill the bottom of the image with flowers, first click the Layers palette's "Add a layer style" icon and select Bevel and Emboss, but don't press OK yet.

7 Click the Layer Style's Pattern Overlay option, and click the arrow to the thumbnail's right to show a palette of currently loaded patterns. Click on the palette's menu triangle at its top right, and select "Nature Patterns." Choose some flowers, and click OK.

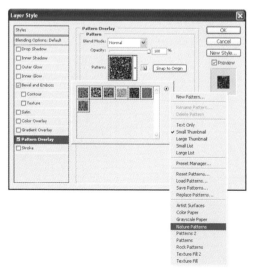

8 In Klimt's greatest paintings, his subjects were wrapped in ornate cloaks. Add a new layer and position it below the Base in the layer stack. Activate the regular Lasso tool and make a tall, roughly rectangular selection. Make the selection's edge less rough with **Select > Modify > Smooth**.

9 Repeat steps 1–5 to make the cloak appear golden, but use lighter shades of brown—try RGB values 255 225 148 and 155 133 68. Before deselecting, click **Layer > Masks > Reveal Selection**—we will use this shape in step 13.

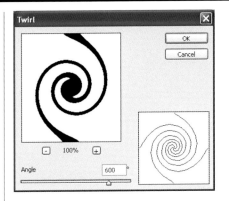

10 To create the patterning, you will need to make some custom brush shapes. In a new file, paint a black line on a white background and use **Filter > Distort > Twirl** to make it into a spiral.

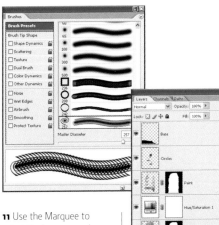

11 Use the Marquee to select the key area and choose **Edit > Define Brush Preset** to create a brush shape. Define 4 or 5 more brushes in the same way. The Brushes palette shows your new presets.

12 Return to your main image and add a new layer. Call it "Paint," then copy the layer mask from the Cloak layer by Alt/Opt + dragging the mask's thumbnail to the new layer. Now, working on the new layer, paint patterns with your new brush shapes, varying the brush size and using various grays for square shapes, and rich reds and blues for circular ones. Continue until the whole area is richly decorated.

13 To make the cloak's decoration more flowing and perhaps more feminine, click the chain on the Paint layer so that the mask is unlinked, then choose **Edit > Transform > Warp**. Drag the points on the grid—here I pulled them inward—and then hit the Enter key.

14 Open the file containing the face. Drag its image layer from the Layers palette and drop it in the main window. Add a layer mask by clicking the "Add layer mask" icon in the Layers palette, and paint away pixels that don't need to appear in the composite image. Here I also switched the layer's blending mode to Multiply, making it blend in better with the gold layers beneath.

15 Finally, make the face visible by activating the Stone layer's mask, and paint black with a hard-edged brush so the face shows through as if it is peering out of a hood. You might also paint a little more on the Base layer so that the figure has a crown of flowers. Decoration is the key to the style.

This project is quite unusual in this book, as the original photo has all but disappeared.

137

Catalan Art Nouveau

The Catalan architect Antoni Gaudí has inspired generations of sculptors, artists, garden designers, and visitors to Barcelona. Sometimes placed within Art Nouveau, Gaudí had initially trained in metalwork and shared the movement's fascination with new materials and fluid forms, which he incorporated into his buildings. Yet he was also a conservative and deeply devout artist who owed as much to earlier Roman and, particularly, Islamic traditions—decorating his buildings' fantastic swirling shapes with mosaics of unparalleled imagination.

Gaudí's decorative style was extremely ornate and varied. His buildings include all sorts of weird, organic shapes—like helmets or the wind-sculpted hoodoos of Utah—often covered with multicolored tiles. Sometimes the mosaics were of small squares, neat and Classical in style, but he also mixed broken tiles, both plain and decorated, with many shapes and colors, and laid them in stripes and patterns, glistening with glass and mirrors.

This Las Vegas Sphinx has exactly the sort of fluid, organic shapes that Gaudí loved. In this recipe, we'll mimic his style, using features found in Photoshop CS2.

1 Open the image. Create a new layer (Ctrl/Cmd + Shift + N) and use the Brush tool (B) to paint some rough stripes in colors that match the image.

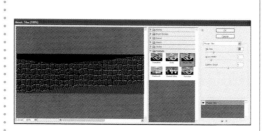

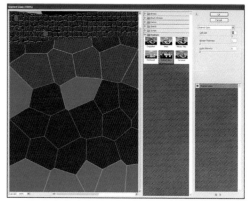

2 Gaudí used a lot of mosaic, so use **Filter > Texture > Mosaic** on one of the stripes you just created (select it with the Magic Wand to localize the filter's effect). Experiment with the tile size and other options.

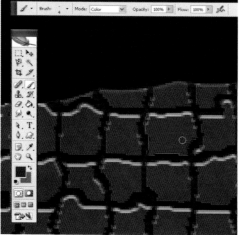

3 Although the tiles are ragged, the Mosaic filter's result is a little repetitive. One way to jazz it up is by painting with the Brush tool. Zoom in close and set a small brush size. Also, set the tool's blending mode option to Color so the tiles' shapes are untouched and only the color changes.

4 The Stained Glass filter is much better suited to imitating a larger, more chaotic style of mosaic. This filter uses Photoshop's foreground color as the "lead" between the "glass" pieces, so first set the foreground to a gray or beige color that looks like tiling cement. Select an area to apply the filter to with the Magic Wand tool (W), then select **Filter > Texture > Stained Glass**. Set a high Cell Size and click OK.

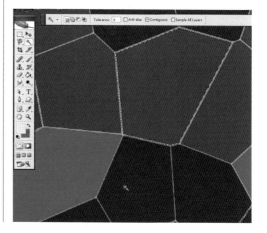

5 Activate the Magic Wand again, zoom in on the new tiles, and click one of them. You may need to set the Magic Wand's Tolerance to a low value so it doesn't select the tiling grout. Then hold down Shift and click a few others to add them to the selection.

6 Apply the Stained Glass filter again, but this time choose a smaller Cell Size, breaking up the selected tiles.

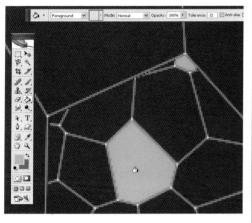

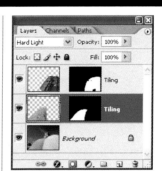

7 Select other tiles, activate the Paint Bucket tool, and click on the tiles to paint them. Use slightly different shades of the same color and paint groups of neighboring tiles, as though the originals had been damaged and you had to replace them.

8 Paint one or two tiles with very different colors—I painted some of mine white.

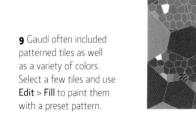

9 Gaudí often included patterned tiles as well as a variety of colors. Select a few tiles and use **Edit > Fill** to paint them with a preset pattern.

11 In Free Transform mode, you can introduce some perspective by holding Alt/ Opt + Ctrl/Cmd + Shift and dragging at a corner.

12 The Free Transform tool's Warp option lets you stretch a layer as though you are laying a wet plastic transfer onto a solid object. Click on it to display a grid. You can drag any of its lines to twist the image, and can also pull at the handles that appear from each corner. At any time, you can click the Warp icon and toggle between the regular and warping transformation modes.

13 When the warping and transformation is close to the required shape, click the Apply icon in the Options bar or hit the Enter key. Fine-tune the result by adding a layer mask and paint it black where you want to hide the tiling and white where it should show. Add other areas of tiling in the same way and experiment with the layers' blending modes. I found Vivid Light worked best for the second patch of tiling. Also, once the tiles are in position and in perspective, you can change the color with the Paint Bucket tool or **Edit > Fill**.

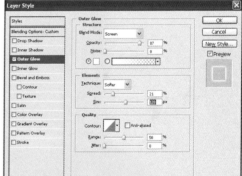

139

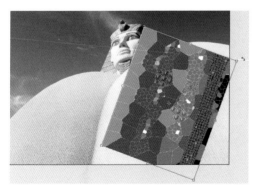

10 Now you need to position the tiling. Choose **Edit > Free Transform** (Ctrl/Cmd + T) and drag the handles that appear around the layer. Here I positioned it roughly over the sphinx's toes and placed the cursor at one corner, rotating the tiling layer.

14 For a final touch, imitate the mirrored tiles Gaudí used. Paint one or two white tiles on a new layer, then switch the layer's blending mode to Lighten and click the "Add a layer style" icon in the Layers palette. Select Outer Glow and increase the Spread and Size.

Photoshop's Mosaic and Stained Glass filters can produce fantastic tiling, and its Warp tool lets you stretch the tiles into any imaginable shape. Gaudí's style is way over the top, so don't be shy.

Cubism

Over a period of seven years leading up to 1914 and the outbreak of the First World War, Cubism marked a decisive break from representative painting, reflecting a radical fissure in politics, art, and culture. Led by Pablo Picasso and Georges Braque, the Cubist painters pursued an abstract, geometric approach.

Cubist paintings often look as if the subject has been constructed from a hundred or more snapshots, all taken from different angles. Where people are represented, they are sharply angular and feature masks that strongly suggest an African influence. Familiar objects, such as violins and guitars, are sliced up and the reassembled fragments skewed and rotated; they are often accompanied by lettering and musical notes. Color sometimes remains, though grays and browns predominate.

140

Using a photograph of an old guitar and a simple background, no special effort was required other than using a high sensor speed (ISO) so that the camera could be hand-held under dim lighting conditions.

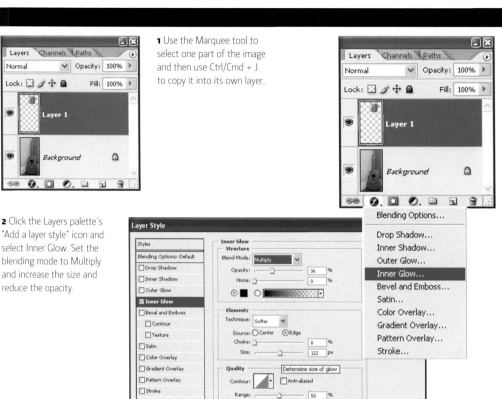

1 Use the Marquee tool to select one part of the image and then use Ctrl/Cmd + J to copy it into its own layer.

2 Click the Layers palette's "Add a layer style" icon and select Inner Glow. Set the blending mode to Multiply and increase the size and reduce the opacity.

3 To give the new layer a different angle, Ctrl/Cmd + click the layer in the Layers palette to select its non-transparent pixels. Choose **Edit > Free Transform** and stretch the layer by dragging any of the bounding box handles. Alternatively, rotate it by moving the cursor just outside the corner and dragging when the cursor changes into a curved, two-sided arrow.

4 To skew the layer, hold down the Ctrl/Cmd key and drag a corner when the cursor changes to a solid arrow. When the layer shape looks right, double-click inside the bounding box or press the Enter key.

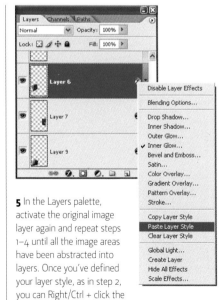

5 In the Layers palette, activate the original image layer again and repeat steps 1–4 until all the image areas have been abstracted into layers. Once you've defined your layer style, as in step 2, you can Right/Ctrl + click the layer in the Layers palette and copy the Layer Style. Paste the style to other layers as you create them.

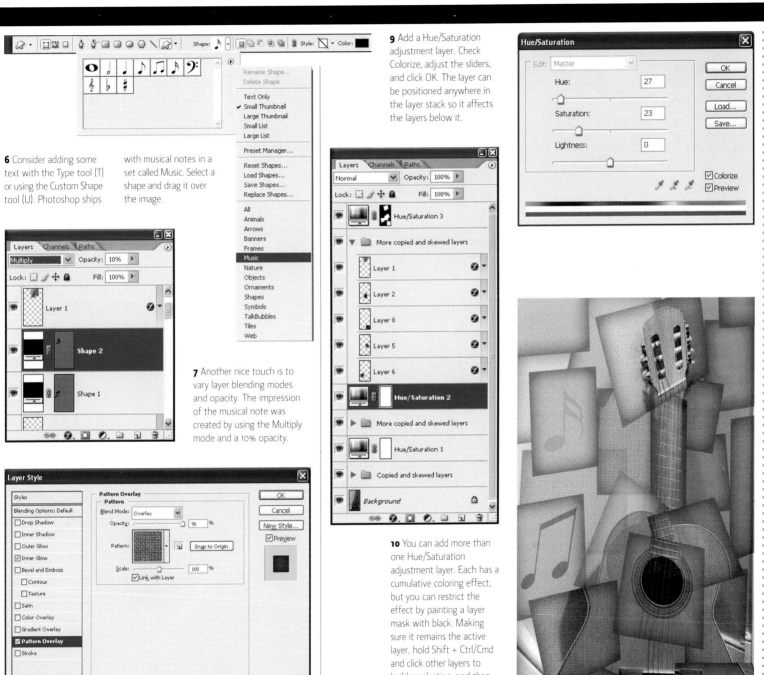

9 Add a Hue/Saturation adjustment layer. Check Colorize, adjust the sliders, and click OK. The layer can be positioned anywhere in the layer stack so it affects the layers below it.

6 Consider adding some text with the Type tool (T) or using the Custom Shape tool (U). Photoshop ships with musical notes in a set called Music. Select a shape and drag it over the image.

7 Another nice touch is to vary layer blending modes and opacity. The impression of the musical note was created by using the Multiply mode and a 10% opacity.

8 At any point you can double-click the layer in the Layers palette and change the Layer Style. Experiment with Pattern Overlay and other modes. If you want to use your chosen style on other layers, remember that from Photoshop version CS2 you can to use the Shift and Ctrl/Cmd keys to select and target multiple layers.

10 You can add more than one Hue/Saturation adjustment layer. Each has a cumulative coloring effect, but you can restrict the effect by painting a layer mask with black. Making sure it remains the active layer, hold Shift + Ctrl/Cmd and click other layers to build a selection, and then fill it with white.

A very ordinary photograph has been transformed into a Cubist image by slicing the original into 25 layers and applying a variety of Layer Styles.

141

Expressionism

Artists have always used painting to express their inner feelings, but with the Expressionists this was far more explicit. Partly inspired by Van Gogh, they were mainly concentrated in Germany and included artists such as Emil Nolde and the Norwegian Edvard Munch. They were not interested in representative painting; they used coarse strokes of vivid, unrealistic colors in their somewhat stark paintings, woodcuts, and lithographs.

Munch produced both painted and lithographed versions of his most famous works, but they share a number of features. The pictures aren't pretty; they are stark with strong, dramatic lines. Many of Munch's works include figures of people, often colored symbolically—white dresses for purity, red for desire, black for death. Suffering and poverty were other themes of a style that was intended to shock.

I chose this picture for its strong and simple shapes—just the man's head and the out-of-focus background. Subtle images with lots of detail would not be appropriate for this style.

1 You need to work on each key image area separately, so use the Magnetic Lasso tool to draw around the out-of-focus background. Simply click and move the pointer along the edge of the face, then around the edge of the image. Press Ctrl/Cmd + J to copy the area into its own layer.

2 Reduce the colors in the new layer by applying **Image > Adjustments > Posterize**. Set the number of Levels to below 10.

3 Apply **Filter > Stylize > Find Edges**. The layer should be converted to a colorful line drawing.

4 Ctrl/Cmd + click the Posterize layer in the Layers palette, click the "Create new fill or adjustment layer" icon, and select Threshold. Drag the triangle beneath the histogram until rough lines start to appear.

5 To make the lines smoother, activate the Posterize layer and blur it with **Filter > Blur > Gaussian Blur**. Use low values.

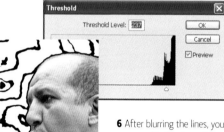

6 After blurring the lines, you may need to fine-tune the Threshold adjustment. Make the lines bold and dramatic.

7 In the Layers palette, temporarily hide the original image, then hold down the Alt/Opt key, and select Merge Visible from the Layers palette's menu.

142

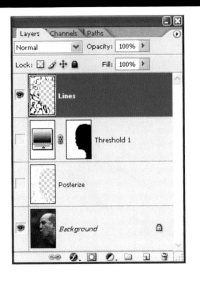

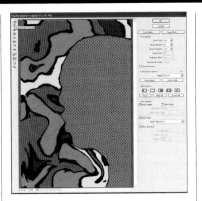

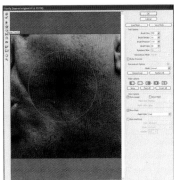

14 Faces may require other techniques and improvisation. To make cheeks look sunken, use the Burn tool (O) to darken them, or try the Liquify filter again. The Pucker tool sucks in pixels, while the Bloat tool can be used to make areas bulge.

8 Hide the Posterize and Threshold layers by clicking the visibility eyes in the Layers palette.

9 Activate the Paint Bucket tool (G) and set the foreground color to a strong yellow. Click a few white areas on the Lines layer to fill them with color. Change the color a few times and fill all the remaining areas with a color.

11 Without releasing the selection, choose **Filter > Liquify**. Use the tools to drag the pixels around. You can click OK, review the results, and apply the filter a few times until you're pleased with the result.

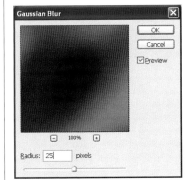

12 Apply a slight Gaussian blur to the Lines layer.

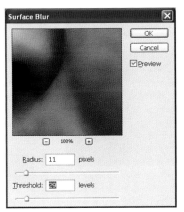

15 You can always reduce the detail in the face by applying the Surface Blur filter (Photoshop CS2 and later) or **Filter > Noise > Median**. You may need to fine-tune your Threshold adjustment layers again.

A simple black-and-white effect emphasizes the man's anger.

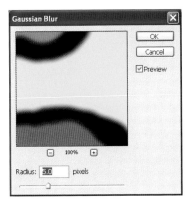

10 Ctrl/Cmd + click the Lines layer and soften the effect by applying a small amount of Gaussian Blur.

13 Apply similar techniques and different colors to the image's other features. Alternatively, you can make a black-and-white "woodcut" version by adding a Threshold adjustment layer (if you're doing this, omit steps 9 and 10).

143

Classical echoes

One of the most prominent of the Fauves (see page 136), Henry Matisse's style was characterized by saturated colors and energetic forms. His work developed in the afterglow of Impressionism, Postimpressionism, and Cubism, and his influences included Classical Greek, Roman, and Persian art.

Around 1910, Matisse was commissioned by a Russian collector to paint a series of works on the theme of music and dance. The results look like the dancing nudes of Greek pottery, but with Matisse's typical unnatural use of strong color. Each figure is reduced to a brightly colored line drawing and set on a plain, bold-colored background.

It's usually easier to extract statues from their background if you shoot them against a clear sky.

1 The first thing to do is remove the statues from their backgrounds. You can try **Filter > Extract** (see Tip box) or use the Eyedropper tool to sample the color and choose **Select > Color Range**.

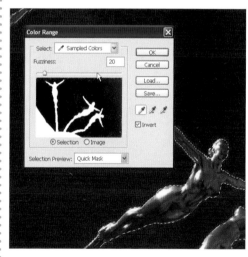

2 The Color Range dialog box shows the pixels that match the selected color. Use the Shift key and click other pixels to add them to the selection, or the Alt/Opt key to subtract them. Adjust the Fuzziness slider and zoom in to be sure you select all the pixels you want.

3 Press Alt/Opt + Ctrl/Cmd + D and soften the selection's edge by 1 or 2 pixels. Then press Delete to remove the background.

4 You can also use the Eraser tool (E) to remove other areas. Again, zoom in close.

Tip

COMPLEX BACKGROUNDS
When the background is not as uniform as a blue sky, try using Filter > Extract instead. Start by using its Edge Highlighter tool to draw a complete outline of the subject (by default, this draws a green line). Mark the area that Photoshop should retain by clicking inside it using the Fill tool, and click OK. Photoshop will then delete the background.

5 Once you have removed the statue's background, simplify the remaining image by choosing **Filter** > **Noise** > **Median**. This blends areas of similar color while retaining the stronger edges.

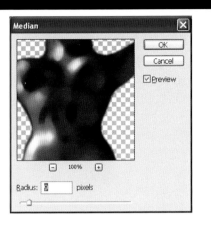

6 Convert the image to a line drawing by selecting **Filter** > **Stylize** > **Find Edges**.

7 Click the "Add a layer style" icon in the Layers palette and select Color Overlay. Set the color to a shade of red and change the blending mode to Multiply. The statue will now be colored red, and its line drawing will show through.

8 Add a new layer (Ctrl/Cmd + Shift + N) and set the foreground and background colors to two rich shades of blue. With the Lasso tool, select an area for the sky and choose **Filter** > **Render** > **Clouds**. If you don't like the first result, Press Ctrl/ Cmd + F and run the filter again—each time you'll get a different, random result.

9 Make another selection for the grass, choose two shades of green for the foreground and background colors, and run the Clouds filter again.

If you can't find athletic friends willing to pose nude for your camera, statues in public places are a great alternative.

10 In the Layers palette, move the statue layers above the blue-green landscape layer. Then use the Move tool (V) to position the image elements in your composition.

The Futurists

Futurism emerged in Italy just before the First World War. It was an abstract style that sought to convey the impression of machines in motion. Cubism was a major influence, as were Eadweard Muybridge's photographs of moving creatures and the emerging artform of cinema. The Cubists showed the subject from many angles, and Futurist artists such as Umberti Boccioni, Giacomo Balla, and Gino Severini took this a step further by depicting various stages of a machine's movement on the same canvas. Futurism had echoes in revolutionary Russia, in the British Vorticists, and also influenced later Art Deco design and the American Precisionist painting style.

Futurist images are frequently so tightly cropped and abstract that you can't easily recognise the subjects. But with the outbreak of the war, many important Futurist works depicted military subjects such as machine guns and armored trains.

Your subject should be mechanical and able to give an impression of speed, movement, and noise. This detail of a steam train is ideal.

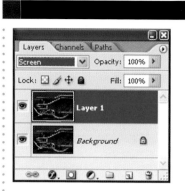

1 In the Layers palette, duplicate your image layer (Ctrl/Cmd + J) and change the new layer's blending mode to Screen. This immediately brightens the image—it's like projecting two copies of a slide onto the same screen.

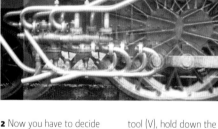

2 Now you have to decide how you want to illustrate the motion. First, we could try duplicate images out of register. Select the Move tool (V), hold down the Shift key, and use the arrow keys to move the Screen layer along the horizontal or vertical planes.

3 With this picture, moving the Screen layer produced an interesting patterning but failed to convey the wheel's movement. It may have worked better if my picture had shown a complete steam train, so it would have appeared to move. A circular movement would suit this image better, so Undo the last step and make a selection of the wheel. Use the Elliptical Marquee tool (M) and hold down both the Alt/Opt key to work from the center, and the Shift key to ensure the selection is circular. Click the wheel's center, and then drag outward.

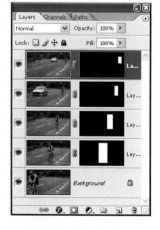

4 For circular motion, a good choice is **Filter > Distort > Twirl**. Enter a rotation angle by dragging the slider or typing in a value. Photoshop makes the selected area swirl. The greatest distortion occurs at the center of the selection; areas on the selection's edges are less distorted. I felt the circular direction of movement suited the subject—the wheel's drive bar punches upward like a right hook, and the spokes create a criss-crossed pattern.

Tip

An alternative "Futurist" method is to mount the camera on a tripod and shoot a series of images. In Photoshop, hold down the Shift key and drag each shot into a single window, then add masks to each and paint around the moving object to isolate it from the background.

146

Save selection as channel

5 When you are satisfied with a selection, it's a good idea to go to the Channels palette and click the "Save selection as channel" icon. This means that later you will be able to Ctrl/Cmd + click the channel and reactivate the selection.

7 Add as many copy layers (Ctrl/Cmd + J) as you need. I added one more layer and twirled it by −150 degrees.

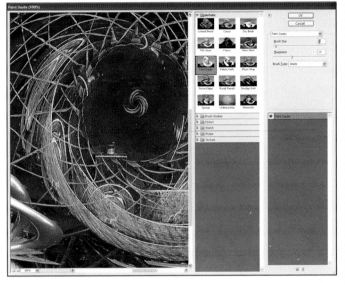

9 To add a painterly effect, consolidate the copies onto a single layer. Hold down the Alt/Opt key and select Marge Visible—in Photoshop CS2, this creates a new layer. Then apply an Artistic filter such as Paint Daubs.

147

Futurist images show multiple, overlapping views of machines in motion. The subject becomes barely recognizable, but there's a palpable impression of speed.

6 To enhance the impression of movement, copy the original image layer by dragging it to the "Create a new layer" icon. Set the layer's blending mode to Screen and twirl or move it again. Here I applied double the twirl that I had used before. If you are moving the layer, using the keyboard makes it easier to move the image precisely—just count the number of times you use the arrow keys.

8 A few Screen layers will greatly brighten the picture, but Photoshop gives you many ways to fix this. Try changing the copy layers' blending modes to Lighten—this immediately restores the darker image areas and shows the lighter swirls. Experiment with other blending modes or add a Curves adjustment layer at the top of the layer stack. Pull the curve down to darken the picture.

Surrealism

PAINTERS & PRINTMAKERS

Surrealism emerged in the 1920s and came to be symbolized by a group of painters who created dreamlike images inspired by the psychoanalytic work of Freud and Jung, and the concept of the subconscious mind. Dali, Magritte, and Tanguy painted individual objects in a highly realistic manner, but "melting" them or placing them in impossible scenes. These paintings remain extraordinarily popular.

Creating a Surrealist image in Photoshop entails selecting items from various photographs and assembling them in one image window. Everything hinges on your choice of objects, how precisely you remove them from their original background, and the way you manipulate them in your new composite image. Dali and Tanguy often depicted exceptionally flat, featureless landscapes and liked to use plenty of visual trickery, so Photoshop's Gradient and perspective transformation tools are invaluable for this project. The Warp command in Photoshop CS2 extends the distortion possibilities even further.

I started with a clock, some eggs, and another image window that was completely empty.

1 Eschewing Photoshop's standard selection tools—the Marquee, Lasso and Magic Wand—I chose the Magic Lasso to isolate the clock face. This tool was more suitable in this instance because it creates a selection that clings to the nearest well-defined edge. I dragged inside the clock's

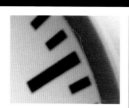

grey rim, rather than on its face, so the Lasso wasn't distracted by the numerals.

2 The Pen tool is good for selecting round shapes like the eggs. Pen-based selections are smoother and more naturally curved. It is tricky at first, but the key is to alternately click and then drag. Click once, drag at a tangent, then click the next

point on the curve, and continue doing this until you've traced all round the object. Here I started by clicking the egg's left side, dragged straight up until the Pen was level with the point I planned to click next, and then clicked that point.

 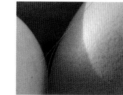

3 When you've traced all round the object, click the first point to close the path. Immediately go to the Paths palette and double-click the Work Path to save it and assign it a name.

4 The path will not be perfect, but you can refine it with the Direct Selection tool. Drag parts of the path, and a handle appears which you can adjust to change the path's angle.

Feather Selection

Feather Radius: [8] pixels

5 Once the path is accurately defined, Ctrl/Cmd + click it in the Paths palette, making a selection from the path. Choose **Select** > **Feather**

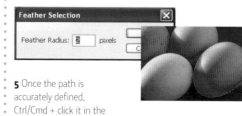

or Alt/Opt + Ctrl/Cmd + D to soften the selection's edges by 1 or 2 pixels.

6 Activate the Move tool (V). Drag each object into the main image's window and use the Move tool to position them.

7 Use **Edit** > **Free Transform** or Ctrl/Cmd + T to resize your objects. Here, the egg layer's "bounding box" is visible; drag one of the corner handles to enlarge it.

8 The new Warp command in Photoshop CS2 is ideal for reshaping image areas. Choose **Edit** > **Transform** > **Warp** to display a

transformation-style box with handles similar to those of the Pen tool. I dragged two of the points where the lines intersect.

9 It's not always easy to transform an object into the desired shape with a single Warp command. Press Enter to apply the initial warp, review your work, and then

warp it again. I wanted my clock to be egg-shaped, so I used the Warp command, then Move, and then Warp three more times.

Save Path

Name: Egg

OK   Cancel

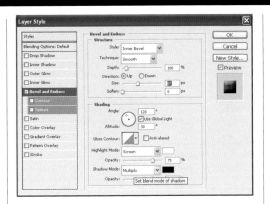

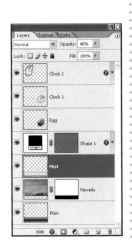

14 Add a new layer for the plain and place it at the bottom of the layer stack. Then make a rectangular selection and use the

Gradient tool to color it. Here I set Photoshop's colors to two shades of brown and dragged upwards inside the selection.

15 You can smooth the transition between the real landscape background and the artificial plain by using layer masks and painting on new layers. Here I softened the bottom of the Nevada layer by adding a mask and painting on it, and then used a soft-edged brush to paint blue along the horizon.

10 Changing a layer's blending mode can really help you see what you're doing. I changed the Clock layer's blending mode to Multiply. This also meant

that when the clock was finally egg-shaped, it looked as though it was painted onto the egg, exactly the appearance I sought.

12 Try applying Layer Styles to your composition: double-click the layer in the Layers palette and experiment. I added a very obvious bevel

to exaggerate the second clock's bean shape. I also added a Custom Shape, a long rectangle, beneath it.

13 For the background, drag another image into the picture and use **Edit > Free Transform** to size it. Here

I used a shot of a skyline in Nevada and left some space for a flat, featureless plain in the foreground.

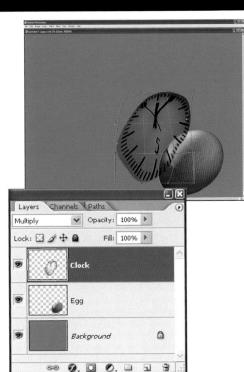

11 The Liquify filter is also very useful for Surrealist effects. Choose **Filter > Liquify**, select one of the tools from the top left, and drag pixels around as though you are manipulating

wet paint. You can use the Warp and Liquify tools in combination—I added a second clock and used Warp to make it bean-shaped, then Liquify to alter small areas.

"Egg Timer." Creating a Surrealist image requires careful use of selection techniques, plenty of distortion tricks, and a vivid imagination.

Escher-style portraits

The Dutch artist M.C. Escher, best known for his woodcuts and lithographs—particularly those of "impossible" geometric structures—made some interesting engravings in the 1950s in which a face or other round object resembled apple peel that has been removed in one long cut. This is a fun technique based on that idea, and you can apply it to all sorts of pictures; but you do need to ensure that none of the subject's edges are cropped out.

Round subjects work best with this effect—balloons, fruit, and portraits that show the top of the head.

I sampled part of the image and defined it as a pattern using Edit > Pattern.

This unusual cloud formation seemed to be an appropriate background for this rather surreal project.

1 Copy the background layer with Ctrl/Cmd + J, call it "Peeling," and hide the original image layer by clicking its visibility eye.

2 You need to remove much of the background, especially behind the head. One good way is with **Select > Color Range**. Here I clicked a pixel in the sky with the Eyedropper tool, then added to the selection by holding Shift and clicking other nearby pixels. Adjust the Fuzziness slider until you can see the correct area is selected. Click OK.

3 Click the "Add layer mask" icon in the Layers palette. A mask is added, leaving just the main figure visible.

4 Paint with the Brush tool (shortcut B) onto the layer mask to hide any other areas.

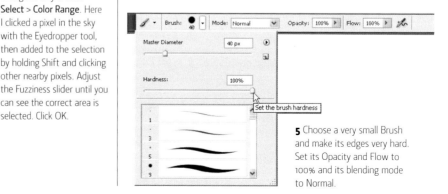

5 Choose a very small Brush and make its edges very hard. Set its Opacity and Flow to 100% and its blending mode to Normal.

6 Activate the Peel layer's mask and paint with a black, slightly diagonal line across your subject's face.

7 Insert a layer directly below the Peel layer and paint the peel at the back of the subject, again with a hard-edged brush—the color is irrelevant. I find it easiest to draw lines first, and then fill them in. Here, I've drawn the lines and am midway through painting in between.

8 In the Layers palette, click the "Add a layer style" icon and select Pattern Overlay.

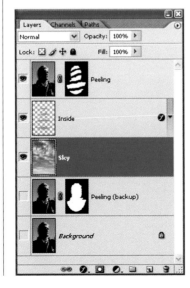

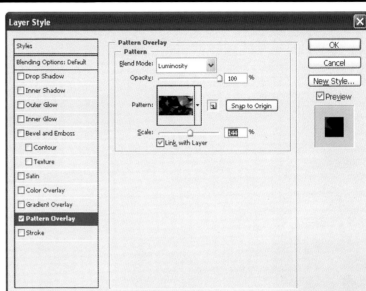

9 Select a pattern and experiment with the other settings. I used the flag pattern I had already defined, but could just as easily have used any other preset pattern. I chose the Luminosity blending mode so only the shapes would show—it's well worth experimenting to find the results you want.

10 To finish the project, drag in another image below the two layers of peel. I chose a sky that seemed to suit the mood of my picture.

What better way to unwind than to experiment with this effective and fun Photoshop technique?

The abstract watercolor

Abstract painting is not just about the rich colors of oil paint. Many Modernist artists, like their predecessors, test compositions and work out ideas in watercolor. Some artists even prefer its apparent simplicity—so much so that they make watercolors their finished work.

In general, watercolors are much less detailed than a photograph's precise record of a scene; colors are subdued and tend to wash together. Forcing a photograph to imitate a Modernist watercolor is likely to involve simplifying it by merging its colors, so choose pictures with clearly defined areas that will be able to accept a lot of Photoshop painting and filters. This is another effect that benefits from being printed on art or textured paper.

I felt this picture's structure could take a Mark Rothko-style blocks-in-the-sky treatment and still echo John Marin's coastal pictures.

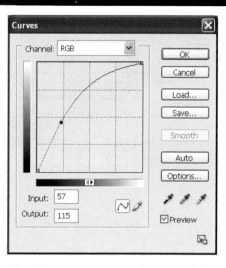

1 Open the starting image. In the Layers palette, click the "Create new fill or adjustment layer" icon and select Curves. Click a point on the curve and drag it upward, making the image much brighter.

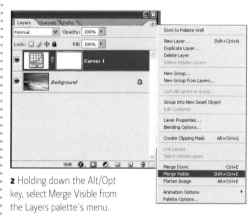

2 Holding down the Alt/Opt key, select Merge Visible from the Layers palette's menu.

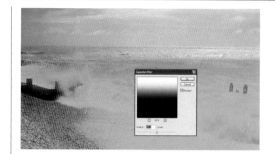

3 Select an area of the image and enter Quick Mask mode (shortcut Q). Select **Filter >** **Blur > Gaussian Blur** and adjust the radius to soften the selection's edge.

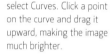

4 Select the Brush tool (B) and choose a brush with an interesting texture via the Brush Preset picker. The Dry Media set of presets is great for adding effects.

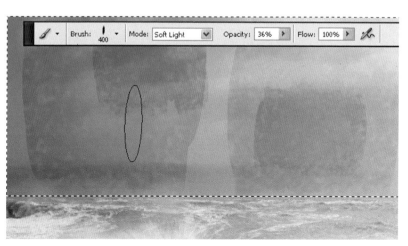

5 Match the brush's size to the area, switch its blending mode to Soft Light, and reduce the opacity. Then paint in the selected area with black. Here I painted three large squares and added a single smaller square to the bottom-right of each one.

6 Once you've finished painting an area, it needs to be made simpler or more abstract. Try the blur filters, or **Filter > Noise > Median**. Here I used the Median filter, and for areas like the sky, which I wanted to solidify, I used a high Radius value. Use lower values where you want to retain more detail.

7 Repeat this process with other image areas. Where the wave is breaking, I only used a low Median filter radius; elsewhere I varied the effects, drawing some lines on the shingle and in the sea.

8 Next go to **Filter > Artistic > Watercolor**, which saturates the colors near edges. Apply it to each selection, or release the selection and use it to give a common appearance that reunifies the image after the various painting effects and Median filters.

9 If you wish, try painting some indistinct shapes freehand. Here I used a small, soft-edged brush and set a low opacity, then added a few lines to hint at a yacht.

10 For a finishing touch, add a soft white border. Place a new layer at the top of the layer stack and use an interesting brush shape to paint white around the layer's edges. Here I clicked in a corner, then held Shift and clicked the next one, and continued around the image.

A series of Photoshop filters simplified and abstracted this picture's main areas before the Watercolor filter applied an overall wash of soft color.

153

Studies of flowers

lowers have always been a favorite subject for painters, and they've been depicted in almost every style imaginable. One relatively modern way to appreciate their beauty is in close-up, where they suddenly become more sculptural and abstract. Painters such as Georgia O'Keeffe were much less interested in depicting reality and more interested in forms, shape, and color.

To create an abstract flower painting, shoot a single flower, extract it from its background, and use its patterns in an abstract design.

Photographing your flower against a plain background makes it much easier to extract in Photoshop.

1 When the petals' edges are clearly defined, it should be easy to separate the flower from its environment. Work on a copy of the image layer (Ctrl/Cmd + J) and select **Filter > Extract**, then paint around its edges with the Edge Highlighter tool. Zoom right in, and set the Size so you highlight both sides of the edge.

2 Work all the way around the flower until the ends of the highlighting line meet. Then select the Fill tool and click inside the area.

Click OK and Photoshop will erase the remainder of the image (hide the original image layer so you see just the working layer).

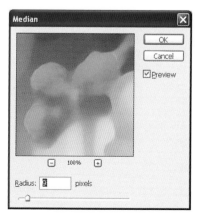

3 The flower is still a little detailed and not abstract enough. Try **Filter > Noise > Median** or the Surface Blur filter, which is available in Photoshop CS2 under **Filter > Blur**. Both methods remove slight gradations of tone while preserving edges. Here I used the Median Filter with a high enough Radius to erase much of the detail.

4 Add a new layer (Ctrl/Cmd + Shift + N) below the flower and use **Edit > Fill** to fill it with a complementary color. This will be the new background color.

5 Duplicate the working layer (Ctrl/Cmd + J) and place the copy below the working layer. Press Ctrl/Cmd + Shift + U to desaturate it. This layer will be used to create a concentric pattern.

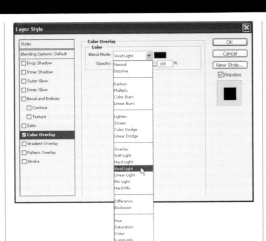

6 Select **Edit** > **Free Transform** (Ctrl/Cmd-T) and stretch the flower by dragging the corners of the transformation bounding box. If necessary, zoom out. The goal is to produce a decorative effect, not a realistic one. When it looks good, double-click inside the box to apply the transformation.

8 In the Layer Style dialog box, click the thumbnail to set the color, then change the blending mode. Use almost any mode—Multiply, Screen, or Overlay are good

starting points—but they're easy to adjust later. Here I used a rich blue and chose Vivid Light, which pumped up the color contrast.

11 There are many other things you can do to fine-tune the image. Try double-clicking a layer and changing the blending modes or adding a Gradient Overlay.

12 Another possibility is to apply various paint-like textures to each layer. Here I applied the Sprayed Strokes filter from the Brush Strokes Filter group, changing the direction on each layer.

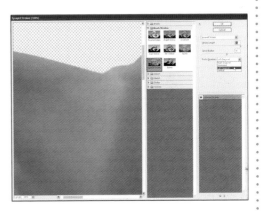

There's no end to the interesting and attractive variations you can create from a single flower shape.

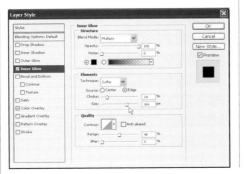

9 Also in the Layer Style dialog, click Inner Glow. Change this property's blending mode to Multiply and its color to black, then drag the Size slider to the right. The idea is to darken the petals' edges and exaggerate the concentricity.

10 Repeat the same process for each of the stretched layers, changing the colors and the blending modes, too, if you wish. To save a little work, copy the style from one layer and paste it to the others by right-clicking/Ctrl+clicking each layer in the Layers palette.

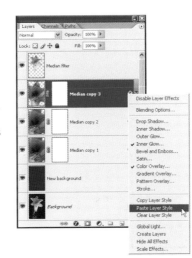

7 Make two more layers and stretch them in the same way. Activate one of them and click the "Add a layer style" icon in the Layers palette, selecting Color Overlay.

The Naïve landscape

Partly as a reaction against the fashionable abstraction of the time, some early 20th-century painters adopted an exceptionally realistic style that celebrated their local heritage and its vernacular. Painting details with an accuracy that sometimes appeared naïve, some, such as the French artist Henri Rousseau, remained amateurs, while others such as the English painter Sir Stanley Spencer were academically trained; the American artist Grant Wood was very cosmopolitan and widely traveled. Each in his own way simplified and idealized the countryside, whether in France, the Thames Valley, or the rolling hills of Iowa.

Many of these "naïve" paintings are almost photorealistic, but they also contain stylized features. Perhaps the most typical is the topiary-like perfection, not just of trees and shrubs but also of crops. In Grant Wood's undulating landscapes, the fields are ploughed and harvested in mechanically precise lines and patterns. Reproducing these is another opportunity to brush up your Photoshop painting skills; but it also requires a surprising application of Layer Styles.

I remember thinking of Grant Wood's 1930 oil painting *American Gothic* when I took this picture—it must have been the couple's slightly stiff, arms-by-the-side pose.

This landscape had some of the simplified elements I sought—rolling hills and distant, striped crops reminded me of Wood's Iowa.

1 Open the start image, create a new file (Ctrl/Cmd-Shift + N), and use **Edit > Fill** to make the whole image layer white.

2 To add the stripes, ensure black is the foreground color and white is the background color. Then choose **Filter > Sketch > Halftone Pattern** and set the Pattern Type to Line. I intended to have wide stripes, so I pushed both sliders up to maximum.

3 Delete the white lines. A quick way is to use Alt/Opt-Ctrl/Cmd-~ [Tilde] to load the layer's Luminosity—in this case, the white lines. Double-click the background layer—so the layer has transparency—and press the Delete key.

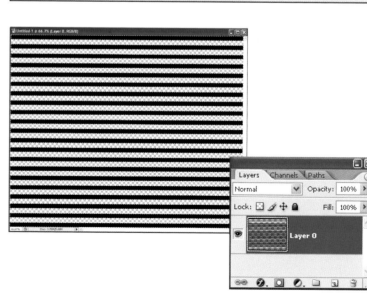

4 Change the layer's blending mode to Multiply, reduce its fill opacity to 20%, click the "Add a layer style" icon, and select Bevel and Emboss.

6 The Stripes layer will need to be resized. Use **Edit** > **Free Transform**, and then drag the handles to stretch the layer, or skew it by dragging a corner while holding Alt/Opt + Ctrl/Cmd. You can also impose perspective by dragging corners while holding Alt/Opt + Ctrl/Cmd + Shift, or rotate it by putting the cursor near a corner until it changes to a double-headed arrow. Here I used all these options to stretch the layer over one of the slopes.

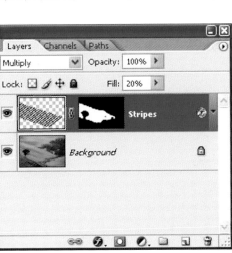

7 Click the "Add a layer mask" icon in the Layers palette and use the Brush tool (shortcut B) to paint black onto the mask, hiding stripes in areas you want to leave unaffected. Here I painted the stripes away from the isolated tree as well as from the rest of the landscape.

5 Drag the Stripes layer from the Layers palette and drop it onto your landscape.

The Naïve landscape, continued

8 At this point some fine-tuning may appear necessary; try adjusting the fill opacity. If the angle of light looks wrong, double-click the layer and change the Layer Style. Here, in the Shading section, I dragged the Angle so that the bevel was lit from the same direction as the landscape.

9 You may also need to stretch the stripes again with **Edit > Free Transform** (Ctrl/Cmd + T). First, preserve the layer's mask by clicking the chain between the thumbnail and mask. To match the undulating slope, use **Edit > Transform > Warp**, which is new in Photoshop CS2. In this tool, drag the lines to warp the "hedges," then press Enter to apply the changes.

10 Add other striped areas by repeating steps 6-11. Vary the layers' opacity. Another trick is to delete rectangular chunks from the stripes area.

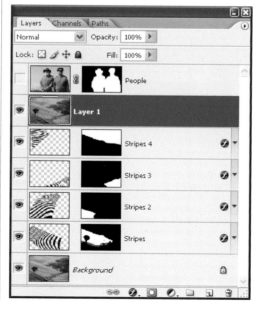

11 At this point, bring the couple into the scene. To make the background less sharply focussed, I temporarily hid the people, and held down Alt/Opt as I chose Merge Visible (in Photoshop CS and earlier, you'll need to create a new layer first).

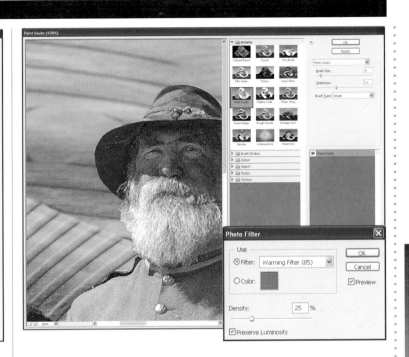

12 Now use **Filter** > **Blur** > **Lens Blur**, concentrating on the way the most distant points lose focus.

14 It's often worth "unifying" a composite image. Either add a Photo Filter adjustment layer or use **Layers** > **Merge** **Visible** and apply the Paint Daubs filter. Don't use high values—some naïve paintings were almost photorealistic.

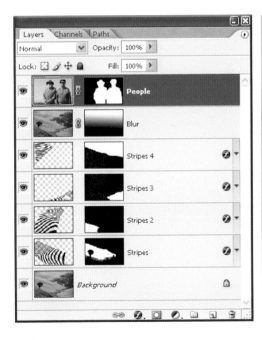

13 Finally, click the "Add a layer mask" icon and drag the Gradient tool to hide the blur in the nearer background.

In marked contrast to early 20th century abstract painting, "naïve" artists turned to representational, photorealistic styles.

Silkscreen style

Almost synonymous with Pop Art, Andy Warhol was a painter, photographer, filmmaker, and publisher. In the mid-20th century he produced iconic silkscreen paintings of subjects as mundane as soup cans and as glamorous as Elvis Presley and Marilyn Monroe. These remain hugely popular, and have sparked countless imitations. Creating your own Pop Art-inspired images with Photoshop is easy, and great fun, too.

The silkscreen technique forces paint onto canvas through a high-contrast negative stencil attached to the fabric. The resulting image features strong blacks from the photograph, which can be simulated using Photoshop's Threshold adjustment. In Warhol's hands, crude blocks of garish, striking color were added to selected areas, and images were often duplicated with alternative color schemes.

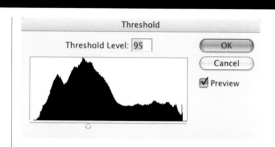

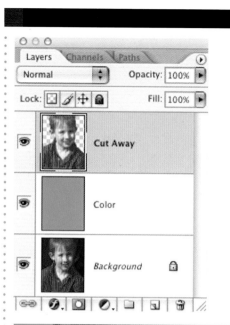

Any portrait can be used for a silkscreen-style image, but those with strong edges work well. Look, too, for an image in which the subject is staring directly at the lens, preferably with a slightly distant expression.

2 To make the high-contrast image, ensure the Cut Away layer is active and select **Image** > **Adjustment** > **Threshold**. Move the slider so that the image contains only enough shadow to show the picture's essential shapes.

1 Open your portrait image, hold down the Alt/Opt key, drag the original image layer to the "Create a new layer" icon, call the new layer "Cut Away," and click OK. Use selection tools such as the Magic Wand and Color Range to roughly select and delete the background pixels from the new layer.

Silkscreen images are very high-contrast, and later steps will remove much fine detail, so you don't need to be very precise. It can make it easier to work if you add a new, color-filled layer directly below the working layer—making it a garish color can help you see the final result.

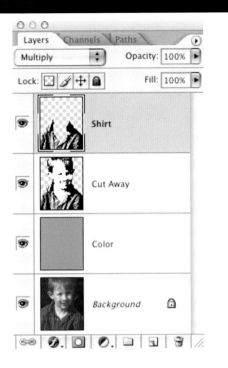

3 Roughly select each image area that you want to paint with a single color, and use Alt/Opt + Ctrl/Cmd + J to copy the selection into its own layer. Name each new layer, set the blending mode to Multiply, and click OK.

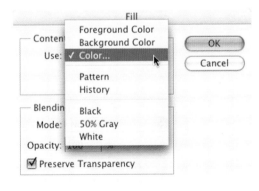

4 Activate each item's layer in the Layers palette in turn. For each one, Ctrl/Cmd + click the thumbnail so that only its non-transparent pixels are selected, and choose **Edit > Fill**. Even if the Fill dialog's Use drop-down shows Color, select it again. This triggers the Color Picker. Select a strong color and click OK twice.

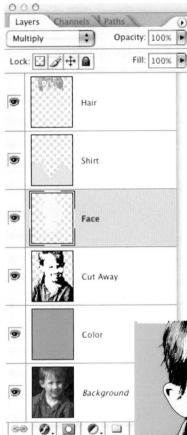

5 In the Layer Style dialog box, change the Color Overlay's blending mode to Color. Pick a strong color and click OK.

6 Once you have repeated steps 4 and 5 for each colored item, you have a completed silkscreen-style image. Save the file and make copies in which you use permutations of the same colors. Each colored area is in its own layer, so it is easy to select and recolor it with a Hue/Saturation adjustment layer. Finally, combine all the versions in one large image.

Combining multiple versions of the same image lends the final version a distinctive 1960s Pop Art feel.

The Pop Art comic strip

One instantly recognizable Pop Art style was inspired by the comic strip and utilized features from commercial and newspaper printing. Roy Lichtenstein painted comic-strip scenes drawn from adventure, romance, or detective stories. Words often appeared as boxed captions along the picture's edge, as speech and thought bubbles, or with huge lettering for maximum impact. And what the words said was important, too—they forced the viewer to ask whether the image was really quite as trivial as its comic form suggested.

In most of these comic strip paintings, the first element you notice is the black line drawing which defines the major shapes in the image. These shapes are colored with either rough blocks of solid color or an even pattern of dots. The palette is usually restricted to red, yellow, and blue—but more shades are introduced by varying the size of the dots and the spaces between them. Closely gathered red dots form a woman's red lips, while skin areas look pink where dots are spaced out more sparsely on a white background. To recreate this style, Photoshop has a few options for converting a photograph into a line drawing. You can then paint onto separate layers, and make some of them dotted with the Halftone Pattern

162

Image quality isn't too important for this technique and you can crop down and use just a small section of the original.

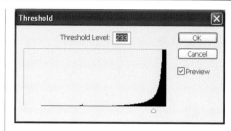

1 Duplicate the image layer and change the new layer's blending mode to Dodge. (You can use the keyboard shortcut Ctrl/Cmd + Alt/Opt + J to do this quickly.) Name this layer "Blurred." You'll soon see why.

2 Invert the Blurred layer using Ctrl/Cmd + Shift + I. This makes the image appear white.

3 The next step is to apply a little Gaussian Blur to the Blurred layer. You will see a colored line drawing start to appear. The beauty of this method is that the blur radius controls the line strength.

4 To remove the color, click the "Create new fill or adjustment layer" icon in the Layers palette and select Threshold. Drag the slider until the line drawing includes all key details, such as the eyes. Because it's an adjustment layer, you can fine-tune it later.

5 You can use more than one Threshold adjustment layer and paint black on their masks. Drag the Threshold slider up to 255 to produce detail in the girl's hair.

6 For each primary color you want to use, add a new layer and change its blending mode to Multiply. Set the foreground color to your primary color and make the background white, then paint on the layer with the Brush tool (shortcut B).

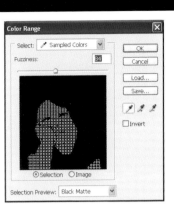

9 A quick way to adjust the layer's color is to reduce the layer opacity, but this fades the color. It's better to increase the white space between the dots, so ensure the foreground color is set to your primary color and choose **Select** > **Color Range**, adjust the Fuzziness, and click OK.

12 As a final touch, use the Text tool to add a caption and the Custom Shape tool to add a thought bubble. Load the Photoshop TalkBubbles set of shapes and drag the shape to the correct size to contain the text.

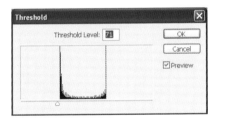

7 To make a colored layer into a halftone pattern, choose **Image** > **Adjustments** > **Threshold** and drag the slider to the left until the primary color disappears. If you look at the layer thumbnail, you'll see the color is now white.

10 With the dots selected, choose **Select** > **Modify** > **Border** and enter a small value, which changes the selection just enough to contain only the edges of the dots. Use **Edit** > **Fill** to paint this selection with the white background color. You'll see the pattern more accurately if you view the image at 100%.

163

Photoshop's Halftone Pattern filter is perfect for creating patterns of colored dots, transforming a photograph into a panel from a comic strip.

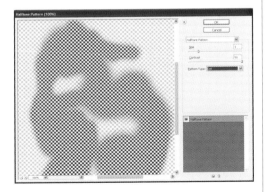

8 Your primary color should still be the foreground color. Choose **Filter** > **Sketch** > **Halftone Pattern**. Set the Pattern to Dot, push the contrast slider to the far right, and adjust the size to match the image area. Then click OK.

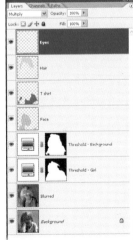

11 Repeat steps 6–10 for each block of color. For areas of solid color, such as the hair and the eyes, you only need to follow step 6.

Swimming pools

avid Hockney would never claim to be a pop artist, but his subject matter has often invited comparison. Born in the United Kingdom, Hockney's style developed when he graduated from the Royal College of Art in London and traveled to Italy and the United States. His exuberant style fused abstract impressionism with traditional painting, the two styles prevalent during his education. However, Hockney's favored subjects owe more to the fact that in 1963, he moved to California, bought a car, drove to Las Vegas, and won enough money to set up a studio.

This project combines multiple layers with the Wave filter to create a sharp, contrast-filled "pool." Creating such a richly detailed pool is the centerpiece of the project, but it only works on a soft, paint-daubed background. There are numerous ways to achieve this, depending on the brush style you prefer. Hockney's style was quite soft—to emulate it, see the tip, bottom right.

The starting image here has no swimming pool, but there is certainly room for one. The feeling of space has been emphasized by keeping the camera horizontal and close the ground.

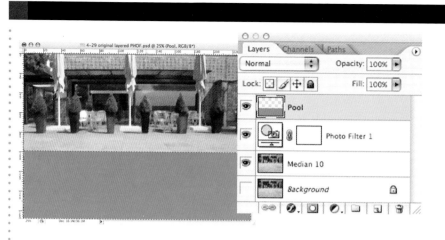

1 Apply a paint effect to a suitable image (see box, bottom right), then create a layer named "Pool." Draw a strong blue rectangle, using the color R50 G151 B222.

2 Open the Layer Style dialog box and add a gradient overlay to the Pool layer, defining a color of R0 G80 B134 in the Gradient Editor.

164

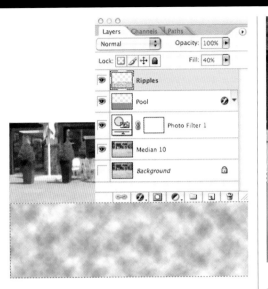

5 Next, make a tiled edge for the pool. Create a new layer named "Tiles." Define an area with the Rectangular Marquee tool and fill it with R126 G197 B247.

3 Use the Pool selection to create a fill on a new layer named "Ripples." Fill it with blue as in step 2. Apply **Filter > Render > Clouds**.

6 Create a new layer named "Tile divisions." With the previous rectangular selection still active, draw a vertical white line 4 pixels wide. With the Move tool, duplicate the vertical white line by Shift + Option + dragging it. Continue duplicating the white line until the width of the tile area is filled. Don't worry about irregular spacing—it adds character.

4 Select **Filter > Distort > Glass** filter. Set the layer opacity to 40%.

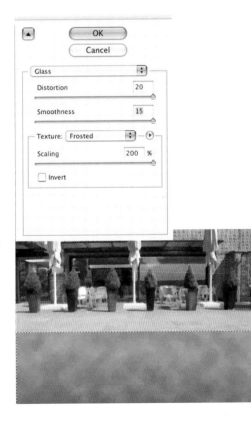

BRUSH DAUBS

To recreate the rich feel of Hockney's paint, use Filter > Noise > Median with a setting of 10. To get the rich Californian tone, apply a warm Photo Filter from the "Create new Fill or Adjustment Layer" button at the bottom of the Layers palette.

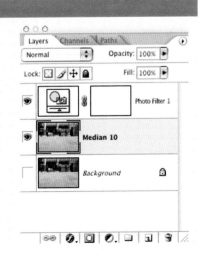

Swimming pools

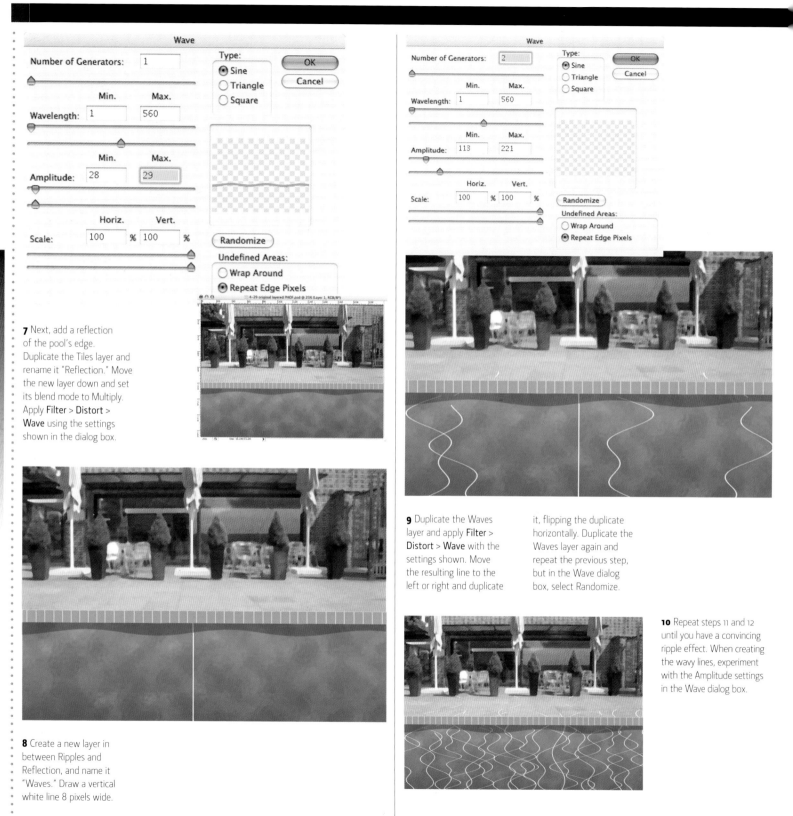

7 Next, add a reflection of the pool's edge. Duplicate the Tiles layer and rename it "Reflection." Move the new layer down and set its blend mode to Multiply. Apply **Filter > Distort > Wave** using the settings shown in the dialog box.

8 Create a new layer in between Ripples and Reflection, and name it "Waves." Draw a vertical white line 8 pixels wide.

9 Duplicate the Waves layer and apply **Filter > Distort > Wave** with the settings shown. Move the resulting line to the left or right and duplicate it, flipping the duplicate horizontally. Duplicate the Waves layer again and repeat the previous step, but in the Wave dialog box, select Randomize.

10 Repeat steps 11 and 12 until you have a convincing ripple effect. When creating the wavy lines, experiment with the Amplitude settings in the Wave dialog box.

11 This process creates a ton of layers, so Shift + click all the layers beginning with "Waves..." (but not the one simply called "Waves") and then select Merge Layers from the top right of the Layers palette. This combines all of the wave layers (except the original straight line) into a single layer. Rename it "Waves combined."

13 Finally, add an edge to the paved area above the pool. Create a new layer, name it "Paving edge," and draw a line 12 pixels wide using a darker version of the paving color. You can complete the effect by adding a drop shadow to the wavy lines.

The completed work has a pleasing, warm background and lines that draw the eye into the image.

12 There may be a few stray lines above the pool area. If so, select the Waves combined layer, draw a selection marquee around the stray lines, and hit Delete.

Glossary

Adjustment layer A specialized layer that can be handled as a conventional layer, but is designed to enact effects on layers below it in the image "stack." These include changes to levels, contrast, and color, plus gradients and other effects. These changes do not permanently affect the pixels underneath, so by masking or removing the adjustment layer, you can easily remove the effect from part or all of an image with great ease. You can also return and change the parameters of an adjustment layer at a later stage.

Alpha channel A specific channel used to store transparency information. Alpha channels can be used to store and control selections and masks.

Aperture The opening behind the camera lens through which light passes on its way to the CCD or film.

Artifact A visible flaw in a digital image, usually taking the form of colored blocks or a noticeable fringe.

Black point An adjustable point beneath the histogram in the Levels tool which can be used to define the darkest tone in an image (beneath which all tones will be set to black).

Blending mode In Photoshop, individual layers can be blended with those underneath, rather than simply overlaying them at full opacity. Blending modes control the ways in which the layers interact, enacting changes on one layer using the color information in the other. The result is a new color based on the original color and the nature of the blend.

Brightness The relative lightness or darkness of a color, measured as a percentage from 0% black up to 100% white.

Burn A method of darkening areas in a photographic print by selective masking. Photoshop simulates this digitally.

Channels In Photoshop, a color image is usually composed of three or four separate single-color images, called channels. In standard RGB mode, the Red, Green, and Blue channels will each contain a monochromatic image representing the parts of the image that contain that color. In a CMYK image, the channels will be Cyan, Magenta, Yellow, and Black. Individual channels can be manipulated in much the same way as the composite image.

Color cast A bias in a color image, either intentionally introduced or the undesirable consequence of a mismatch between a camera's white balance and lighting. For example, tungsten lighting may create a warm yellow cast, or

daylight scenes shot outdoors with the camera's color balance set for an indoor scene may have a cool blue cast.

Color temperature A measure of the composition of light, defined as the temperature—measured in degrees Kelvin—to which a pure black object would need to be heated to produce a particular color of light. A tungsten lamp has a color temperature of around 2,900K, while the temperature of direct sunlight is around 5,000K.

Contrast The degree of difference between adjacent tones in an image, from the lightest to the darkest.

Crop To trim or mask an image so that it fits a given area or so that unwanted portions can be discarded.

Curves A Photoshop tool for precise control of tonal relationships, contrast, and color.

Default The standard setting or action used by an application without any intervention from the user.

Depth of field The range in front of the lens in which objects will appear in clear focus. With a shallow depth of field, only objects at or very near the focal point will be in focus and foreground or background objects will be blurred.

Depth of field can be manipulated in-camera for creative effect, and Photoshop CS2's new Lens Blur filter enables you to replicate it in postproduction.

Dialog An on-screen window in an application used to enter or adjust settings or complete a step-by-step procedure.

Displacement map An image used with filters such as Displace to determine the level and position of distortion to be applied. Any Photoshop PSD file can be used as a displacement map, except those saved in Bitmap mode. The Displace filter uses the first channel in the image for horizontal displacement, and the second channel for vertical displacement.

Dodge A method of lightening areas in a photographic print by selective masking. Photoshop simulates this digitally.

Drag To move an item or selection across the screen, by clicking and holding the cursor over it, then moving the mouse with the button still pressed.

Eyedropper A tool used to define the foreground and background colors in the Tools palette, either by clicking on colors that appear in an image, or in a specific color palette dialog box. Eyedroppers are also used to sample colors in other tools.

Feather An option used to soften the edge of a selection that has been moved or otherwise manipulated, in order to hide the seams between the selected area and the pixels that surround it.

Fill A Photoshop operation which covers a defined area with a particular color, gradient, or texture pattern.

Gradient A gradual blend between two colors within a selection. The Gradient tool can be set to create several types, including linear, radial, and reflected gradients.

Grayscale An image or gradient made up of a series of 256 gray tones covering the entire gamut between black and white.

Graphics tablet A drawing device consisting of a stylus and a pressure-sensitive tablet. Many people find them easier to use than mice for drawing. The pressure sensitivity can be set to different functions, such as controlling the opacity of an eraser, or the width of a brush.

Grayscale An image or gradient made up of a series of 256 gray tones covering the entire gamut between black and white.

Halftone A technique of reproducing a continuous tone image on a printing press by breaking it up into a pattern of equally spaced dots of varying size—the larger the dots, the darker the shade.

Handle An icon used in an image-editing application to manipulate an effect or selection. These usually appear on screen as small black squares which can be moved by clicking and dragging with the mouse.

Hard Light A blending mode that creates an effect similar to directing a bright light on the subject, emphasizing contrast and exaggerating highlights.

High-key image An image comprised predominantly of light tones.

Histogram A graphic representation of the distribution of brightness values in an image, normally ranging from black at the left-hand vertex to white at the right. Analysis of the shape of the histogram can be used to evaluate tonal range.

Image size The size of an image, in terms of linear dimensions, resolution, or simple file size. In Photoshop, we mainly talk about image size by describing horizontal and vertical dimensions (e.g., 1,280 x 1,024), qualified by the resolution (e.g., 72ppi).

Infrared The common name for radiation beyond visible light but shorter than microwaves. Using special filters, traditional cameras could take pictures of the infrared end of the spectrum, which tends to highlight body heat. Many digital cameras are incapable of taking infrared photographs because the sensor technology deliberately blocks infrared "interference"—you can test your camera's response by pointing a television remote control at it, since these are effectively infrared torches.

Lab Color mode An intermediate color mode used by Photoshop when converting from one mode to another. It is based on the CIE L*a*b* color model, where the image is split into three channels, "L," the luminance or lightness channel, and two chromatic components, "a" (green to red) and "b" (blue to yellow).

Layer A feature used to produce composite images by suspending image elements on separate overlays. Once these layers have been created, they can be re-ordered, blended, and their transparency (opacity) may be altered.

Layer styles A series of useful preset effects that can be applied to the contents of a layer. Examples include drop shadows, embossing, and color tone effects.

Layer mask A mask that can be applied to elements of an image in a particular layer, defining which pixels will or will not be visible or affect pixels underneath.

Low-key image A photographic image consisting of predominantly dark tones, either as a result of lighting, processing, or digital image editing.

Midtones The range of tonal values that exist between the darkest and lightest tones in an image.

Motion blur In photography, the blurring effect caused by movement of objects within the frame during the exposure of the shot. Photoshop contains filters to replicate motion blur.

Multiply A blending mode that uses the pixels of one layer to multiply those below. The resulting color is always darker, except where white appears on an upper layer.

Noise A random pattern of small spots on a digital image, usually caused by the inadequacies of digital camera CCDs in low-light conditions. Photoshop's Noise filters can add or remove noise from an image.

Opacity In a layered Photoshop document, the degree of transparency that each layer of

an image has in relation to the layer beneath. As the opacity is lowered, the layer beneath shows through.

Overlay A blending mode that retains black and white in their original forms, but darkens dark areas and lightens light areas.

Pen tool A tool used for drawing vector paths in Photoshop.

PPI Pixels per inch. The most common unit of resolution, describing how many pixels are contained within a single square inch of an image.

Quick Mask A feature designed to rapidly create a mask around a selection. By switching to Quick Mask mode, the user can paint and erase the mask using simple brushstrokes.

Resolution The degree of quality, definition, or clarity with which an image is reproduced or displayed on screen or on the printed page. The higher the resolution, the more pixels are contained within a given area, and the greater the detail captured.

Specular highlight An intense highlight, often resulting from the reflection of an extremely bright light source such as the sun or a lighting reflector. Specular highlights are plentiful in photographs of highly reflective

surfaces such as glass or highly polished metal.

White balance A setting used in a digital photo or video camera to compensate for the varying color temperatures of different forms of lighting. A tungsten preset, for example, will adjust for the amount of yellow light given off by tungsten lighting.

White point An adjustable point beneath the histogram in the Levels tool which can be used to define the lightest tone in an image (above which all tones will be set to white).

Index

Index

Further Resources

GENERAL COLLECTIONS

These major galleries possess some of the world's most extensive searchable online image collections. They provide authoritative commentary on pictures and other educational material.

Their URLs are subject to change—in fact, the Louvre changed its link to English content while I was writing this book—so these links point to home pages which may not be in English. In each case, the home page contains a link to the site's English language content.

EUROPE

British Museum, London	http://www.thebritishmuseum.ac.uk
Hermitage, St Petersburg	http://www.hermitagemuseum.org/
Kunsthistorisches Museum, Vienna	http://www.khm.at/
Le Louvre, Paris	http://www.louvre.fr
Musée d'Orsay, Paris	http://www.musee-orsay.fr
National Museum of Photography, Film & Television, Bradford	http://www.nmpft.org.uk/
National Gallery, London	http://www.nationalgallery.org.uk/
Prado, Madrid	http://museoprado.mcu.es
Rijksmuseum, Amsterdam	http://www.rijksmuseum.nl/
Uffizi, Florence	http://www.uffizi.firenze.it
Victoria and Albert Museum, London	http://www.vam.ac.uk

UNITED STATES

The Art Institute of Chicago	http://www.artic.edu/
George Eastman House	http://www.eastmanhouse.org/
	http://ftp.geh.org/
Getty Museum	http://www.getty.edu/art/
Metropolitan Museum of New York	http://www.metmuseum.org
Museum of Modern Art, New York	http://www.moma.org/
Museum of Fine Art, Boston	http://www.mfa.org/
National Gallery of Art, Washington	http://www.nga.gov/
New York Public Library	http://digitalgallery.nypl.org
Smithsonian Institution	http://www.si.edu/

TECHNIQUES AND STYLES

General

American Memory Project	http://memory.loc.gov/ammem/
R. Leggat's History of Photography	http://www.rleggat.com

Painters & Printmakers

Escher	http://www.mcescher.com/
Andy Warhol	http://www.warhol.org/
David Hockney	http://www.saltsmill.org.uk
Gaudí	http://www.gaudi2002.bcn.es/
Turner	http://www.tate.org.uk

ANTIQUE OR ALTERNATIVE PROCESSES

General

http://unblinkingeye.com/

http://www.mikeware.demon.co.uk

http://www.contactprintersguild.com

http://www.alternativephotography.com

Specific

Daguerreotype	http://www.hrc.utexas.edu/exhibitions/permanent/wfp/Daguerrotype
	http://www.metmuseum.org/special/French_Daguerreotypes/dawn_images.htm
Calotype	http://photography.about.com/library/weekly/aa052002a.htm
Wet plate collodion	http://www.collodion-artist.com/
	http://www.dunniway.com/
American Civil War	http://www.civilwarphotos.net/
Cartes de visite	http://memory.loc.gov/ammem/
Eadweard Muybridge	http://www.kingston.gov.uk/museums
	http://photo.ucr.edu/photographers/muybridge/
Autochromes	http://www.autochrome.com
Frank Meadow Sutcliffe	http://www.sutcliffe-gallery.co.uk/

TWENTIETH CENTURY

Man Ray	http://www.manray-photo.com
Tina Modotti	http://www.comitatotinamodotti.it/ctm.htm
Edward Weston	http://www.edward-weston.com/
Ansel Adams	http://www.anseladams.com/
Bill Brandt	http://www.billbrandt.com/
	http://www.vam.ac.uk/collections/photography/brandt/index.html
Herman Leonard's jazz photography	http://www.hermanleonard.com

STREET, HUMOR, AND KITSCH STYLE

Ellitt Erwitt	http://www.elliotterwitt.com
Martin Parr	http://www.martinparr.com/

LANDSCAPES

Rolfe Horne	http://www.f45.com/
Michael Kenna	http://www.michaelkenna.net/
Infrared photography	http://www.simonmarsden.co.uk
Robert Mapplethorpe	http://www.mapplethorpe.com/
Polaroid techniques	http://www.kathleencarr.com/
	http://www.goinggallery.com/
	http://jackperno.com/
Surreal photography	http://www.danburkholder.com/

Bibliography and Acknowledgments

Bibliography

The Art of Photography, Mike Weaver (ed),
   Yale University Press, 1989

The Story of Art, E.H. Gombrich, Phaidon, 1995

Polaroid Manipulations, Kathleen T Carr, Amphoto, 2002

Photoshop Masking and Compositing, Katrin Eisman,
   New Riders Press, 2004 (This book covers advanced
   techniques for selecting and extracting objects.)

Acknowledgments

Thanks to the people at Ilex for giving me the opportunity to write this
book. I hope it will give readers a fine excuse to visit their favorite art
galleries, as well as provide those moments of inspiration when you realize
you've just found the way to create your own "Van Gogh" or "Ansel
Adams." Your appreciation of the artists will not be diminished.

This book is dedicated to my mother, who still inspires so much, and
to my family, particularly Ann and Allan Williams, Allan and Jane, Tom,
Alice, and Sophie. Also Denise, Manuela, Chi—who I'm sure always
believes in me—and Adrian. Thanks also to Sue and Antony, Ian Curtis,
and Sir Alex Ferguson.